The Mystery of Anwards in Tidenham Parish

Diana Cave

Copyright © 2024 Diana Cave

All rights reserved, including the right to reproduce this book, or portions thereof in any form. No part of this text may be reproduced, transmitted, downloaded, decompiled, reverse engineered, or stored, in any form or introduced into any information storage and retrieval system, in any form or by any means, whether electronic or mechanical without the express written permission of the author.

The views expressed in this work are solely those of the author and do not necessarily reflect the views of the publisher, and the publisher hereby disclaims any responsibility for them.

Front cover image:
Isaac Taylor's map of Gloucestershire 2nd Ed. 1800
(Kind permission of Gloucestershire Archives ref. MA19/24)

ISBN: 978-1-917425-83-4

PublishNation
www.publishnation.co.uk

*To all in the parish of Tidenham:
past, present and future.*

ACKNOWLEDGEMENTS

I would like to thank the many people who provided information and support for this book.

Thanks to all those I have talked with and their contributions even if I do not know your names. However, here are some local names that I do know: Ann R., Jan & Keith B., Carol & Richard C., Cate P., Celia & Ollie H., David, Jean & Derek C., Elizabeth, Emma D., Grace T., Josie & Dave G., James & Julia P., Janet, Keith U., Lew, Liz M., Non, Wendy Merrick.

In the wider area there are many more to thank for access to their records that enabled me to carry out more research.

Ancestry.co.uk. Bergen Maritime Museum, John Burrows for information about the Chepstow Bridge and an Admiralty Chart. Chepstow Society. Richard Clammer. Gloucestershire Family History Society. Paul Evans, Senior Archivist, Gloucestershire Archives, (Gloucestershire Heritage Hub). Geoff Gwatkin. Liz McBride (Beachley information). Marilyn (Moon & Co.). National Library of Wales. Tidenham History Group. Keith Underwood for The Photograph!

Finally, this book would not have been completed without two special people. They have been with me all the way through the ups and downs of historical hunting.

Mike, my husband, who has supported me with ideas, field-work, measurements, great computer help, photographs, photographic editing, deciphering inventories, analysis of the book content, proof reading, and his sketch view of the area.

Andrew Lillington, for introducing me to new subjects, other on-line research sources for information, N.L.W. research, apple information, proof reading, suggestions, encouragement and the Gloucestershire Archives visits.

Finally, E. & O.E. I've checked references many times, but everyone is fallible.

CONTENTS

INTRODUCTION 1
CHAPTER 1 THE BEGINNINGS 8
CHAPTER 2 LIFE IN THE 1600's 15
CHAPTER 3 STRANGE TIMES 23
CHAPTER 4 ALL CHANGE IN THE 1800's 37
CHAPTER 5 CROSSING THE SEVERN 56
CHAPTER 6 TWENTIETH-CENTURY EXTRACTS 73
CHAPTER 7 'THE NOW SHALL OUR MORROW INSPIRE' 85
CHAPTER 8 CONCLUSION 91
ACKNOWLEDGEMENTS FOR PHOTOGRAPHS 101
BIBLIOGRAPHY 102
GLOSSARY OF TERMS 104
MAPS 106
WEBSITES USED: 2022-2024 107

INTRODUCTION

The first thing you may be thinking is what, where or who is Anwards? The answer is easy, it was once a house or mansion that seems to have disappeared. However, that raises many more questions, and after researching for more than three years using maps, books, documents, local people's knowledge, together with field-work, the past has given up some of its secrets.

It might be helpful if Tidenham Parish is described; clarifying its locality for anyone unfamiliar with the area, new residents, visitors or explorers.

This westerly part of Gloucestershire bordering Monmouthshire is roughly wedged shaped with the River Severn on the east side, and the River Wye on the west. It tapers to Beachley peninsula. The parish consists of the following settlements in alphabetical rather than in size order: Beachley, Boughspring, Sedbury, Stroat, Tidenham, Tidenham Chase, Tutshill, Wibdon and Woodcroft. Hundreds of years ago there were isolated larger houses with small peasant ones nearby to service their needs. However, this parish like others changed with more houses being built for industrial workers in Chepstow or further afield.

At the end of this Introduction, you will find a map of 1828 showing the beginning of some of this change through outlines of building plots for sale in Tutshill by the owner Osborne Yales, Esq. Look at the map and you can see the crossroads, the junction of Coleford Road, Gloucester Road, Beachley Road and Castleford Hill. The former Cross Keys pub is not there, although a few buildings are marked. Tutshill was no more than a hamlet then. However, the Weighing Engine or weighbridge is clearly visible as is the Turnpike Gate, which must have been a good source of income in the early nineteenth-century. A few of the plots had been sold. It may be of interest to know the names of these new owners. Lots 6 & 7 Willett, Lot 5 Samuel Gunn, Lots 3 & 4 Richard Morris, Lot 8 James Price, Lot 11 John Williams, Lot 18 Thomas MacCulloch, Lots 1 & 2 Mr Fryer. If more information is required about this map the reference number below the photograph gives the source at Gloucestershire Archives, which is abbreviated as G.A. and the number following gives the reference number to use when accessing Gloucestershire Heritage Hub. The abbreviation G.A. will be used for all future reference sources in this book.

The Ordnance Survey (O.S.) map of 1844-1888 1st edition shows Wirewoods Green, although you may have noticed that the Isaac Taylor map on the front of this book has the name as *Wyrhall Green*. This house or manor in 1769 had a long avenue of trees connecting it with Gloucester Road. An impressive entrance for visitors. Do any of the trees remain? It is likely one does, namely the yew tree at the junction of Elm Road with Gloucester Road. The Forestry Commission issue guide lines for woodland owners on how to calculate tree ages by measuring the girth. This is dependent on the type of tree. Our calculations put the age as 268 years, measured in 2022. This shows growth began in 1754. Allowing a decade or two for error this tree seems a remnant from Wirewood's past. Indeed, yews are remarkably long lived. There is one in Fortingall, Perthshire that is reputed to be thousands of years old. In fact, a high proportion of churchyards have yews, although this may reflect the activities of early Celtic saints or even earlier pagan people and their symbolic relationship with these trees.

In the quest for Anwards more discoveries have been made about the people who lived in this parish, which is interesting as it helps to bring the past alive. It is a salutary reminder that although it was centuries ago the people had the same needs then as now, for example money and grievances. Also, documents reveal what they valued, which was very different from that of today. Land management has changed too and this is discussed in the book.

This book consists of eight chapters with a brief explanation of each to follow.

The first chapter explains the reasons for the interest in Anwards together with evidence of its location in the parish. The names on a group of gravestones in Tidenham churchyard are discussed as they are associated with Anwards. Other sources of information are mentioned.

Chapter 2 begins by considering many significant events that presumably affected rich and poor alike. This is followed by a closer inspection of the first branch of the Webleys, the family connected with Anwards. An idea of what goods and chattels were deemed important to them is given by using extracts from inventories. This is included to give a closer understanding of the early sixteen hundreds. Land is purchased for probably many reasons, so examples are given.

Chapter 3 considers the group of gravestones in more detail. Many facts are also included about The Mead following the death of one of the Webleys, to be subsequently followed by the rebuilding of this house. Some of the problems caused by this decision are mentioned. A reference to the situation of Anwards is included.

In Chapter 4 maps are used to explain features, countryside problems, and describes land for sale, which gives more details about the site of Anwards. Details are given about George Ormerod and his daughter Eleanor. A brief examination is made of parts of the Census' from 1841 to 1891 together with railway developments.

The River Severn is the focus for Chapter 5, and a detailed examination of a potential passage is considered together with possible reasons for this crossing.

When the Romans exercised control of England, there were probably many river crossings in the locality, so reasons and locations are suggested. Roman archaeology in the parish is considered, together with their settlement and port in Bristol. An example is given to show how difficult it is to calculate locations when few named places are given.

An analysis of what has been discovered about Pighole Pill is considered together with its probable origin as a route crossing. Some problems faced by those living near the Severn are discussed together with land purchases in this parish. A short reference is made to some of the types of boats and ships used to navigate these sometimes-turbulent waters. Possible hermits associated with the islet of Beachley are considered, and Eleanor Ormerod's dimensions for the chapel are mentioned.

The twentieth-century is the subject for Chapter 6. In fact, this may be of more relevance to local people than some aspects of earlier chapters. However, past decisions, whether political, economic or whatever, reflect how many live here now. Again, the Census' are briefly examined from 1901 to 1921, and also the land and buildings that were for sale in 1927. The 1939 Register for Anwards Cottage and nearby properties are discussed as are many changes in the locality. For example, Sedbury Park, the new Severn Bridge, more houses built and also the slight, but significant change in direction of the A.48.

Chapter 7 is short as at the time of writing only 24 years have passed for this century. However, mention is made of more house building, the brief effects of COVID-19, and several new developments for outdoor activities etc.

The final chapter is the Conclusion, which draws together the known evidence, analyses some information that is probably relevant, and suggests possible answers to this mystery of the disappearing house.

At the end of the book there is a bibliography, a glossary for any unknown terms, the maps used, and on-line reference sources.

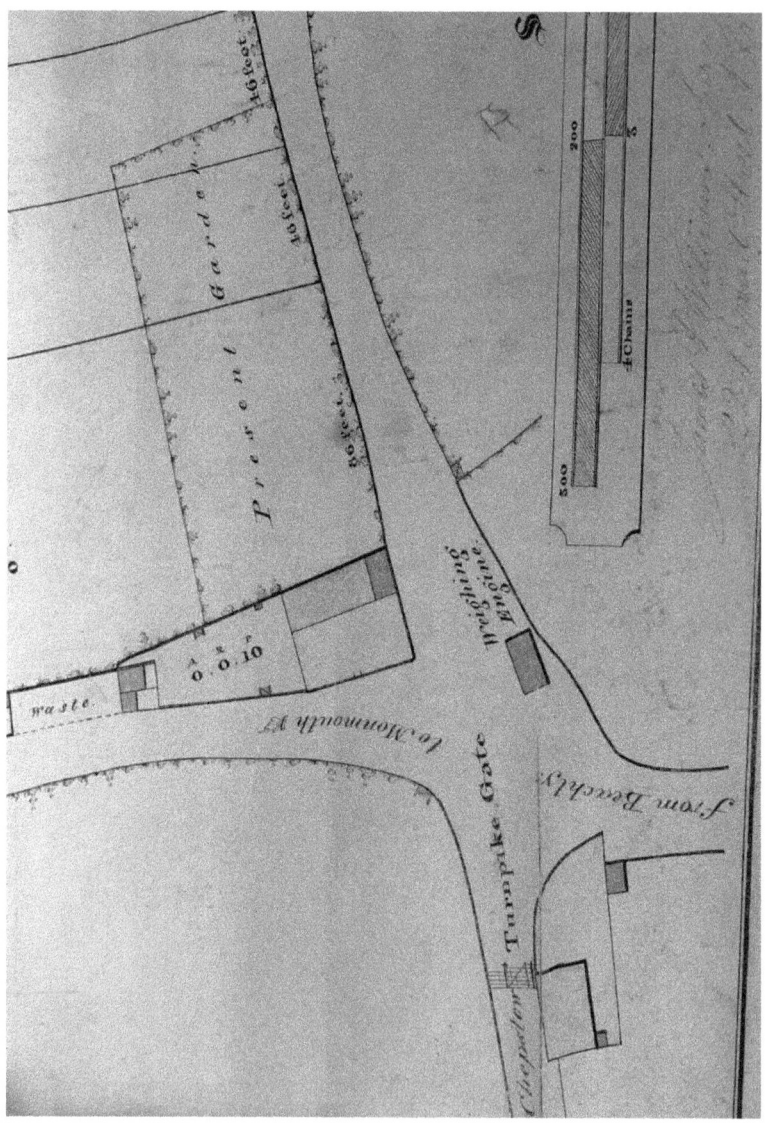

Plan of lands, Tutshill 1828.

Yew Tree, Gloucester Road, Tutshill.

CHAPTER 1

THE BEGINNINGS

The mystery of Anwards began when helping to clear the graveyard of vegetation at St Mary & St Peter, Tidenham in 2021. Years of neglect had allowed brambles and other creeping plants to run riot. Slow progress was made, but eventually many of the headstones revealed who was buried there. Local family names occur, and often they are in a group of relatives. Many lived long lives and others sadly short ones. However, the views from the church across the Severn to the distant hills are uplifting and may have comforted the bereaved. It is unlikely that these views have changed much, apart from Oldbury former power station. The wide sweep of the river, the Vale of Berkeley, the distant Cotswolds and the expanse of sky give a wonderful panorama.

There is a group of chest tombs by the path leading from the lychgate to the church entrance on the southern side. This is where the name Anwards appeared on one tomb and Annords on another. The family name was Webley, so that was another source to investigate. Also, there seems to be many names for the house too. There is an Anwards, Annards, Annords, Anards, Anwells and even the Census Enumerators recorded differences, Hannards (1851) and Hanards Cottage (1921)? All this seems to indicate either a lack of hearing, or accent misunderstanding, or literacy on the part of one or more stone masons, or a clerical error.

On closer inspection of these Webley tombs, there are also other names between the graves. There are Watkins', and on the slab above a Webley grave there is John Smart. Plenty to investigate there it would seem. Unfortunately, the weather, mould and lichen have made some letters illegible on the graves, and in some cases parts of the carving has crumbled away. However, all is not lost as Ralph Bigland (b.1711/12 d.1784) collected memorial inscriptions throughout Gloucestershire. He eventually became Garter King of Arms.

In order to find out more about Anwards, the house, it is important to go far back in time to see when the house name or building first appeared. The earliest tomb mentioning Anwards is 1717, yet that is the third grave back from the path. A titled grave northward before this one, mentions 1712 for a William Webley. The next grave is adjacent to the path, but appears to be sunken so if there were inscriptions on the sides, they are not visible, and assuming they still exist. Perhaps there was some sort of void below caused by water ingress that caused the subsidence, and maybe there were several burials made on top of each other.

The only way to try to find any earlier Webleys is through the death and burial records. Fortunately, there were two 'Williams' buried in Tidenham, one in 1657 and the other in 1670. It seems probable that the sunken chest tomb was in a similar state when Ralph Bigland was recording inscriptions in the mid seventeen hundreds. He makes no mention of a 1657 or 1670 Webley gravestone. However, he did record information about what he found inside, in the chancel of Tidenham Church. 'In memory of Hannah, daughter of William, Grandson of William Webley who was the son of Walter Webley, Gent, interred here abouts 1630'. It would seem that this memorial stone and grave is likely to be under the encaustic patterned tiles much loved by the Victorians. However, his information gives confirmation that the Webleys were in the area in the seventeenth-century, and Anwards appears to be their place of residence.

An attempt was made to trace Hannah Webley without success. The problem is a lack of documents, combined with too many 'Williams' and 'Walter' Webleys resulting in a maze of families, and no definite conclusion as to which branch was correct. It is probable that the best chance of success would be to look closer at William Webley who died in 1657, because it is possible that he is buried in the sunken tomb by the church path.

The approximate location of Anwards is easier to see, although in later chapters maps are examined and show that the house appears to have moved to where a cottage was. On the front cover of this book is part of one of the maps of Gloucestershire surveyed by Isaac Taylor, 1800 2nd Edition (G.A. ref. MA19/24). You can see a house marked 'Annards' in the Sedbury area near to the River Severn. Another house nearby, but unmarked, is probably The Mead. Wyrhall Green is shown as is 'Tiddenham' along with the church. However, larger houses are shown too, namely Jones Esq in Tidenham and Hill House, so Annards must have been a smaller house. Beachley is also marked, as is the islet there, named as Chapel Rock.

The Great Map of the Severn Estuary c.1595 mentions Betesley (Beachley), Slyme Roode, Inward pille and Cune pille. It is possible that Inward may have originally been Anward.

Ordnance Survey maps are helpful in following footpaths as sometimes routes on the ground are not clear. There is a list of O.S. Maps at the end of the book, but the O.S. Explorer Wye Valley & Forest of Dean OL 14 2015 shows Anwards House, and this location will be discussed in depth later.

Documentary evidence appears to indicate that Anwards was in existence in 1498/9, but how much reliance should be placed on this evidence is questionable. For a start, the titled 'Ancient Deeds of Franklyns Tenement' document reveals it was written on the reverse of a railway timetable! This gives a mirror image, but it is decipherable to show the following, 'RailWAY TIMETABLE April 1891' and places such as London, Oxford, Leamington, Chester and Manchester. However, what is shown are useful location factors and dates, so extracts will be used occasionally to highlight aspects.

The first reference in the document is dated 'March 20.14.H7-1498/9 original parchment'. The H7 refers to Henry 7th (b.1457 d.1509). This shows '…between the land held by Walter Philpot on the north, and the common way leading from Sudbury cross to Anwells…' Two things to note here, Sedbury was once Sudbury or Suddebury, and Anwards seems to be Anwells at an earlier date.

Some of the byways became hollow ways, often the result of wear and tear, but they offered shelter in inclement weather. The lane from the medieval cross at Sudbury, which passed Anwards was called Bird's Lane. The Bird family existed in the parish, although no record has been found linking them to this lane.

George Ormerod (b.1785 d.1873) was an antiquarian and historian who moved from Cheshire to Sedbury in the 1820's. He wrote a paper called 'Strigulensia', Striguil being an old name for Chepstow. He also mentions Anwards 'From the higher or northern landing-place on the Severn, another ancient way leads by the site of Anwards or Anwells…' referenced in the 1499 deeds. But since his paper was written before the information composed on the 1891 parts of a railway timetable mentioned above, it indicates that Ormerod might have seen the original documents. He also uses the word 'site', which means where something was or is, so it seems likely a building or a ruin was there. It seems pointless to put the name on the chest tombs in the eighteenth-century if Anwards was a ruin.

The next chapter is about the sixteen hundreds, nearly four hundred years ago, and gives links to Bristol and a little of what life was like for the Webleys.

Webley tombs at Tidenham Church.

Sunken lane at Sedbury.

CHAPTER 2

LIFE IN THE 1600's

This chapter sets the scene about what life was like in the 1600's, as well as finding some clues about Anwards, and with more mysteries about the Webleys.

There were so many unexpected and unsettling events during this century, which would have affected the rich and poor alike. The change in royalty from Elizabeth I (1533-1603) to James I (1566-1625), then Charles I (1600-1649 with the regicide), followed by Oliver Cromwell, the Lord Protector (1599-1658), and finally the return of Charles II (1630-1685), probably confused many. There were yet more changes after 1685, but these examples will suffice.

Health and death were unpredictable too, with the Black death or Bubonic plague epidemics, for example in 1593, 1625 and especially in London in 1665. Smallpox and other virulent diseases were a problem too.

Political intrigues were rife with many of the population taking sides. The 1605 Gunpowder Plot, although more than one hundred miles away, may well have led to dissension. Of course, the Civil War, 1642-1651 surely affected the locality with Royalists or Parliamentarians needing food, water, shelter etc.

Then there was the 1607 flood, which affected low-lying areas of the Bristol Channel and the Severn. Many people and livestock drowned, and the medieval reclamations of large areas for pasture were overwhelmed. Some think this was caused by a tsunami, but a fierce storm combined with low pressure, prevailing westerly winds and spring tides after the new moon could be the culprit. It sounds similar to the 1953 floods along the East Coast of England and along the Thames.

One important fact to mention is the harvest failures from 1647 to 1650. The crisis was again caused by the weather: storms, unpredictable frosts and excessive rainfall. Many people were starving in 1649 and there was stealing of corn in the Severn Valley. England was affected badly by the extremes, such as summer rains in 1648, then summer drought the following year. Indeed, a vicar in the Gloucestershire Parish of Hartpury said in 1647 'We suffer dearth, if Warrs renue/Twixt the twoe Kingdomes, both shall rue.' (G.A. ref P165/IN/1/1).

Returning to the Webleys and their link with Anwards. The first problem was working out their origins. Had they always been in this parish, and the documents to prove this are yet to be discovered? Or did they move to the western fringes of Gloucestershire because it offered more protection rather than comparatively nearby cities? There was a William Webley d.1614 from Brockworth, a yeoman, and other Webleys in Gloucester, but no convincing linking evidence has been found. However, Bristol is a possibility, and if the weather and tidal conditions were right it was a comparatively easy and fast option to get to the other side of the Severn.

Fortunately, a discovery in Gloucestershire Archives about the Webleys, helped in understanding why certain documents were created. A Walter Webley is the earliest Webley found, yet there is still no certainty as to their origins.

To expand further, a Walter Webley made a Deed of settlement dated 20 September 1618 of '…messuage…divers lands…Parish of Tiddenham, alias Tudenham, settled on said Walter Webley for his life', then to 'Anne for her life' and to 'William Webley for his life', after their death. But a later document, Abstract of title to the Mead Estate, is dated 16th February 1628. This date is significant. It was the date for the planned wedding of Walter and Anne's son William to Dorothy Hollister. It seems the parents were concerned in case it did not take place. Walter was leaving one part of the estate to Anne, and the other part to William, then the whole estate to the wife of said William at his death. Phrases such as 'intended marriage' and also 'moiety', a part or portion, to 'William Hollister, Edward Hollister and John Hollister one moiety of said premises.' It might have been to protect any heirs as it was entailed.

Two later discoveries appear to confirm that this branch of the Webleys had come from Bristol, either through ancestors or marriage. A William Webley died in 1657, but he married Dorothy Hollister on 16th February, 1628 at All Saints', Compton Greenfield, South Gloucestershire. But intriguingly directly beneath the entry in the church records it states John Hollister married Margaret Webley presumably on the same day, although two words following in the record are indecipherable as they appear to be abbreviated. There is no record of this marriage from another source.

Much more information is found in the 1657 will. William was an 'Esquire' of Tiddenham. He had three daughters and two sons and used an interesting phrase for his wife Dorothy, namely 'my now wife'. Did this mean he had been married before? However, it might show they had been courting for a while or it was just legal jargon, which is the most likely reason.

For some time, William had been buying land in Tidenham Parish: 100 acres including fields named such as Little Mogor's Leaze and Great Grove etc., from someone called Edmond Hopkins (?) Gent. He also bought five acres of wood from Thomas Llewellyn (Lewellings) of Tiddenham on 29th April 1646. There was a purchase between William and William Cann, Esq. of Bristol regarding some land in the parish of Henbury, Manor of Compton Greenfield, and that was left to his youngest son William in William senior's will made in 1654.

On 18th April 1656 an Indenture was made between William and Dorothy Webley and Henry his eldest son in 'special Tail'. What does that mean? Apparently, there are many different types of tail, and it is a way of owning property that can only be passed down to specific family members, for example a child. The document mentions a messuage, copse and much land situated in Sudbury that was purchased by Walter of John Goughe, Mary his wife and Thomas his son. It was 'To hold to said Henry, his heirs and assigns for ever.' These documents are difficult to read as there is vertical writing in brown ink on the sides too.

An Indre Tripartite dated 21st April 1656 was made between Henry Webley of Tydenham, Gent. 1st part, Richard Hawkins of Symonds Inn, Middx, Gent. 2nd part and William Webley, Robert Smith of Hill, Gloucestershire, yeoman and William Hollister of Redwick, Almondsbury, yeoman, 3rd part. This document mentions arable or pasture land called Lewellyns Lane Leaze and two tenements called Anwards and Lewcroft. This is the first time Anwards has been mentioned in a document connected with the Webleys. It states 'that Capital house and all the lands thereunto belonging called Anwards', which was left to son William. William senior died in 1657, but in spite of searching for documentary evidence and gravestone inscriptions nothing has been found. His whereabouts and that of his wife remain a mystery.

The next person on this quest to find out more is also a William Webley, Gent., died 1670. Evidence shows that this William was the son of William who died in 1657, as mention is made of Compton Greenfield and his uncle William Hollister, his mother's brother. No mention is made of Anwards, so probably his mother, Dorothy, was still living there during 'her natural life', which ended in 1674.

Interestingly, there is an Inventory of 1670, presumably of William's goods and chattels, which give an idea of what they valued, used and deemed as important. A few examples and their worth are mentioned. (G.A. ref. GDR/R10/53).

	£	s	d
9 piggs & one 'smaller' one	08	04	00
corns up on the ground	25	20	10
the middle chamber 3 beds 3 bedsteads 3 bolsters 3 ruggs & one course hedd 6 blankets and one chest	12	00	00
flocks of bees	01	00	00

Appraised by Edward Collins and Thomas Watkins.

At the beginning of this chapter a brief overview was given about many of the threats faced by the local populations. It is possible that William dying comparatively young in 1670, may have been infected by a disease when travelling around Compton Greenfield and other settlements in the area. Also, did the Civil War affect them? No evidence of any pertinent action either Royalist or Parliamentarian has been found, and it is unlikely there was anything to entice any search in a probably remote area. On the other hand, there were two battles at Beachley and two sieges of Chepstow quite nearby, so nothing is certain. But there is evidence of coins being buried near Stroat, just in Tidenham Parish. This Tidenham Hoard contains coins from 1560 to 1642 with a mixture of shillings, one very rare one from Shrewsbury, then sixpences, half-crowns and one gold Unite of 22 carats. Perhaps someone was trying to avoid robbery and intended to return shortly, but unfortunately never did. These coins are housed in Chepstow Museum.

Finally, evidence from a map dated 1643/1646 by Janz Blaeuw, Amsterdam, gives a few more details about this parish. Tydenham is marked with its church. Wullaston and Lancante are indicated as is The Treacle (islet) off Beachley, although the latter is called Settesley pass. The bridge to Chepstow is also marked.

The next chapter has much more information about houses, people, places and of course the somewhat confusing Webleys.

All Saints', Compton Greenfield.

CHAPTER 3

STRANGE TIMES

Webley and Anwards in the 1700's are difficult to follow. It starts off relatively simply with a William Webley chest tomb at St Mary & St Peter's Church, Tidenham. The carvings are legible, considering the side facing the church is dated to 25th May, 1712, and he died aged 56. Adjacent to this epitaph is a message: *'Nothing there that can pretter (Latin meaning beyond or more than) The Stroke of death when time is spent Therefore my frinds (sic) prepare to die That you may Live Eternally.'*

The east side of the tomb shows what is presumably the Webley Crest indicating that he was a Gentleman. Trying to describe a coat of arms is not easy, although there is a photograph at the end of this chapter. The Arms show '3 mullets of 6 points…A mailed arm…a hand grasping a dagger'. The motto is 'Perseverance'. For additional information, a star with straight-sided rays is normally known as a mullet. The description of the Arms can be found in 'The Welshman & General Advertiser for the Principality of Wales, 21st February, 1890', page 6. The southside of this grave states Walter Webley his son departed this life 18th or 13th March 1763 aged 68 years.

There is no mention of Anwards. Documentary evidence is scarce and the will seems to be a standard printed one, with spaces left to put in details. Eleanora Webley, widow,

William Webley late of the parish of 'Tiddenham', 1712 are written and signed by Ellinor Webley, Kedgwin Hoskins and another. There are at least three different spellings of her name, but it is the same woman. This is probably caused by clerics, the family, a stone mason or even Eleanor herself.

Then 'Elinor' died in 1715 and this time it is Walter, the son of William Webley of Sudbury who fills in brief details, or a scribe. Elinor's grave is adjacent to the north of William's, died 1712, and is a much lower apparently slab tomb. The height may be for many reasons, and as mentioned earlier there could be other family graves beneath. The name Sudbury is mentioned and it is possible that William, Elinor and Walter were living in The Mead off Sedbury Lane before they died. Fortunately, there is a detailed Inventory of the goods and chattels of Mrs. Ellinor Webley of Sudbury made by Appraisers John Robert and Thomas Dale 23rd May 1715. This is very comprehensive even including debts due from Mr. Henry Davis, Thomas Brown, William Gilbert, Jane Robinson and William Jenkins. Names have been included in case they help genealogists.

Here are some examples what the Webleys used, their worth and what was deemed important.

	£	s	d
Two dozen and a half napkin,			
nine pillow cases,			
four Three pairs of sheets	03.	00.	00
Nineteen dishes of pewter	03.	07.	00

Three guns	01.	00.	00
Nine bushels of malt five bushels of oates with two bushels of pease & one bushel of 'gegsoy' seeds	02.	08.	06
In the 'cellars': eight hogsheads of syder & two hogsheads & barrel of vinegar	10.	10.	00
Ten acres of good wheat @ £2.50 an acre	25.	00.	00
Five acres of indifferent barley	05.	00.	00
Three acres of ordinary pease and a half	03.	00.	00
Four acres of indifferent oats	02.	00.	00
Two acres of beanes	04.	00.	00
Twenty 'tups' (rams) of sheepe	08.	00.	00
Saeven cows & a bull	28.	00.	00
Fifty two year old cattle	15.	05.	00
Six oxen	24.	00.	00
One syder mill press and trough	03.	00.	00
The deceased apparel	30.	00.	00

Since the focus of this book is on Anwards only a brief consideration is made to the other Webley graves in the churchyard to the south of the graves mentioned above. The next grave is inscribed William Webley of Anwards died 1717. From documents the evidence shows he had three daughters, four sons, was married to Jane and was a yeoman. On side two is Christian, their daughter, who died in 1776.

Between the chest tomb above and the next one are two headstones with the surname Watkins. A quick digression reveals that a Dorothy, who died 1728? was the wife of Edmund Watkins. This is likely to be the William, who died 1670, and his wife Christian's daughter. The other headstone is for Nathaniel Watkins, died 1757.

The last chest tomb on Side one facing the Severn, has the inscription: Elizabeth wife of Walter son of William Webley Annords Gent Sept 1728 or 1720, 57 years and for William's son, died Dec 10 1728 10 weeks. Side two facing the church the inscription is for Jane daughter of Walter Webley by Eleanor, his wife of Magett, June the 2nd 1754 aged 5 years. The eastward facing side has the same family coat of arms but without the mailed arm etc.

The slab on top of this tomb is very confusing. At the top is Walter son of William Webley gent? of Annards died May 7 1774/3. Then the next inscription below is for John Smart Oakcliff Nov 12 1887 aged 74 yrs., and below this is Anne relict Jan 5 1890 aged 78 years. However, it is probable that the Smarts, like the Watkins are related by marriage.

To simplify the complexity of this family, it is less confusing to consider only the branch of the Webley family who lived in the Mead, and the Walter who died in 1763.

This is because documents such as the Indenture of Lease below, or 'agreement', give more clarity to the mystery of Anwards.

This Walter Webley had a son called William who was baptised in 1721 at Tidenham. He went on to become a successful lawyer in Chancery Lane, London, and as son and heir was responsible for administering his father's estate in 1763.

The indenture was signed on 1 August (Lammas tide) 1763 between William Webley of Symonds Inn, London, Gent. and Mary and William (her son) Lewis for five and a half years. (N.L.W. citation 550).

The Inventory of fixtures included items that would be necessary for day to day living. For example, in the dairy there was a cheese press and a salting stone, and in the room above there was a malt mill. The buildings consisted of The Mead, barn, stable, cyder mill etc. together with gardens, orchards, meadows and pasture, totalling approximately forty-four acres. Also, included was more arable and pasture land of about twenty-two acres called Millfield, with a further six acres adjoining. Plenty of land for two people to manage.

However, under this indenture Elizabeth Webley, widow and William's mother, strangely appears to be sharing part of her house with the Lewis'. It is possible she needed support and this was a compromise; the Mead property being too large for her.

The Webley family seem to value fruit and nuts, as a detailed reference is made to trees: the Pear and Damson trees, the Great nut tree, the Little Walnut tree etc. There was also a requirement for 'two barrells of cyder of fifty-five gallons' free annually to the Webleys. This is proof that much of Tidenham Parish had large areas of orchards. Indeed, there was also a yearly requirement to produce a better-quality cider, as this quotation revealed 'William Webley his heirs and assigns one barrell of cyder containing fifty-five gallons gratis well made of the best fruit growing upon the said demised premises (styre excepted)'. This apple grew well in the Forest of Dean on the iron-rich soil, and appeared to benefit the kidneys.

It would seem that Mary and William Lewis, the tenants, stayed on for the term and would have to leave by February 1769 (Candlemass), the 'term of five and an half…'.

There is a document of 1764 about Anwards and other messuages in the area, which seems to imply that properties are being sold from William Jones Esq., son, to Robert Pyrke Gent., although this could be referring to tenants or undertenants. (G.A. ref D2957/306/15). Webley property and lands have been mentioned since at least 1654 as being in their ownership, so it is difficult to understand what was happening, but the Webley family definitely owned them in 1770/1. The dates of many of the later Indentures seem to vary, and it is difficult to read the documents in places. Abbreviations add to the problem, as does different handwriting and ink. Also, the clerks copying the documents may have made mistakes, and judging by all the lines through words and sentences, together with arrows to insert phrases or names, and many smudges, this seems to be the case.

William Webley (baptised 1721) was buying land and clearly expanding his ownership in the parish. In fact, for whatever reason he planned for a new Mead House to be built, although it is not certain whether it was constructed around the original house or as part of it. He also borrowed finance for this purpose. Wherever houses are built raw materials are needed, but in the 1700's it would have been much harder to move heavy stone. So where was the source of rock for this construction? One possibility was robbing stone from ruined buildings nearby. The O.S. 25" map 1844-1888 1st Ed. shows an old quarry and lime kiln near Tump Farm, but it is not marked on the 1843 Gloucestershire Tithe map or on the 1840 pre-Gloucestershire inclosures map. However, the latter mentioned map shows that a nearby footpath has been 'stopped up' or closed, so the quarry may have been started later in mid-1850's. Another source could be Anwards itself. That may sound unlikely, but there would have been some dressed stone, and the descent from its site would make transportation easier. The maps mentioned above show that the shape of Anwards has change over the decades.

Before considering the next events in William's life, it is worth considering an earlier map of this part of the parish as it is of the same era. This extract is from part of the map by Isaac Taylor 'County Map of Gloucestershire' 1777 1st Ed., which is a few years earlier than his map on the cover of this book. It is not surprising that this map is creased and shows definite signs of wear, considering the number of people who must have looked at it. The only difference between the two maps is the use of colour making the main road from Gloucester to Chepstow more prominent.

Then something happened to stop William's expansion of his property and lands. He now lived in Chancery Lane in the County of Middx. with his wife and family, and was a well-respected lawyer. It might have been the death of his mother, or an investment failure, but whatever happened the Indenture of 20 November 1770/1 revealed that he was selling the Mead Estate to 'Thos. Nichole of Watford in the County of Hertford, Gent'. It also named a 'messe tenement or dwelling'...'by the names of Anwards'...Also other named pasture fields as well as 'Anwards Grove containing by estimation 2 acres'. There is an interesting name for one 'peice' of land 'Gooty Ground' about 6 acres, which makes one wonder the origins of its name. (N.L.W. citation 551).

In fact, an Indenture of April 1771, abstracted Indré also of 20 November 1770 shows a sum of £3000 between William and the Honourable Lord James Viscount Grimston and his heirs, so presumably a mortgage. However, it is the same date as the proposed sale to Nichole, so was William hedging his bets? This must have been a stressful time for William, so it is not surprising he died shortly afterwards in 1779. He is buried in St Dunstan's, Cranford St John, Hounslow, Middx. as is one of his sons. There is more to be learnt about William the lawyer, his wife Ann (née Sainsbury), who, for some reason, had a clandestine marriage at St Giles, Mayfair in 1752. Their son William Henry had an interesting life, but a brief overview of this family must suffice to avoid deflecting from Anwards over the next few centuries.

William's will, made April 1779, leaves all his properties and estates in 'Tiddenham', Frampton Cotterell and elsewhere in Gloucestershire and Cranford, Middlesex to Ann. He mentioned his 'very dear and only child William Henry Webley'. At first glance it seems they only had one child, but this was not the case, so it means his only surviving child.

William Henry joined the Navy in 1779, when he was only 15, and significantly the year his father died. He married Maria Washington White in 1800 and his naval career eventually led to his promotion to Rear Admiral. In 1815 he inherited Noyadd Trefawr. He died in 1837.

However, a year after William died, ownership of the Mead Estate was on the move once more. 'The Bath Chronicle' of 11 May 1780 was advertising a sale in Bristol of Lots in the Freehold estates of William Webley. Lot 1 'A new-built Manfion-Houfe, called *the Mead*', which gives details of outbuildings, 'a large garden walled round', meadow, pasture and orchards. Surprisingly, fruit trees and a particular type of cider apple are mentioned, so this implies they were important apple trees in the vicinity. This cider apple appears to have vanished, but the soil in the parish favoured such trees. It is the same variety that was mentioned in the 1763 Indenture earlier in the chapter, although the advert spells it differently as 'ftier', which is stier, and perhaps that was how it was spelt in another part of the region. Unfortunately, in 1788 proceedings were begun to recover the £3000 from Ann, William's wife and son William Henry.

However, before the Webleys disappear from this book there is one surprising fact and that involves the Walter Webley who died in 1774. He left an interesting legacy to his nephew's son Edward Webley, namely The Island of Jamaica. Plenty to think about there.

The next chapter with the focus on the nineteenth-century looks at practical issues, changes in life styles and means of transport, the growth in population, and the arrival of the Census every ten years.

Webley Coat of Arms.

Christian's tomb at Tidenham church.

The Mead, fields once orchard.

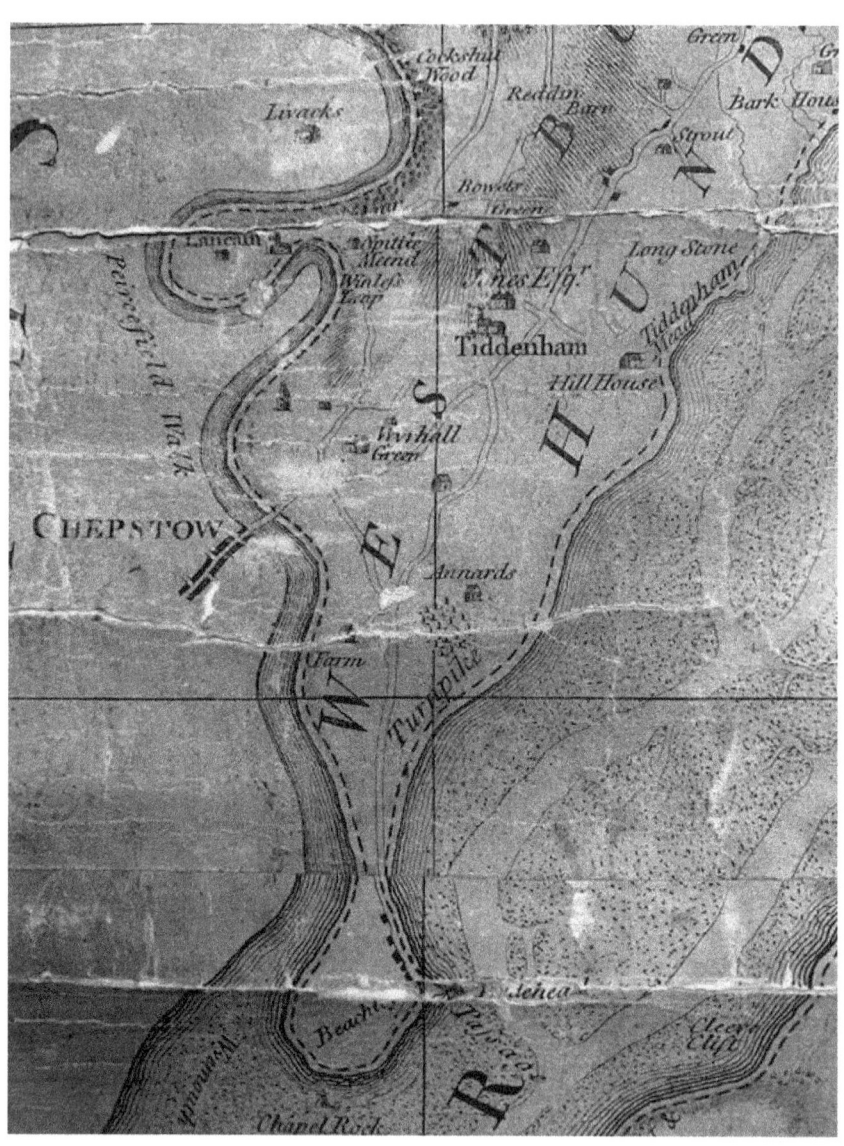

Isaac Taylor, Map of Gloucestershire 1777 1st Edn.

CHAPTER 4

ALL CHANGE IN THE 1800's

Maps are almost like the paths in life with the choice to use the wiggly roads or the straighter motorways. You can follow the latter and reach your goal quickly, unless there are unforeseen circumstances. However, you might miss interesting attractions such as hidden coves, majestic mountains, creepy forests, palaces, heritage railways etc.

The Ordnance Survey published its 1st Edition of the 25 inches to 1 mile for their period 1844 to 1888, and it is useful to compare then with now to see how the landscape has changed. This map has already been mentioned in the previous chapter and if you follow the links mentioned you can also see the 2nd and 3rd editions that give details up to 1939. Use G.A. GDR/T1/182 for the link to see them. It is surprising what can be found, showing how the parish was extensively covered with orchards, and the following is a list of approximately where they once existed. Lancaut, Bowspring, Wallhope Farm, Oakcliff, Stoulgrove, Pinmoyle Terrace, Wirewoodsgreen, Tutshill Farm, Bishton Farm, Cross Hill, Tidenham House, Church Cottage, Day House, Sugar Loaf, Philpots Court, Hanley House, Wibdon Farm, Little Wibdon, High Hall, Wibdon Cottage, Garston, Rosemary Cottage, Stroat House, Stroat Farm, Mead House, Tump Farm, Anwards House, Sedbury Farm, Badams Court, Rose Cottage, Pensylvania, Brick Cottage,

Beachley Farm and Beachley Lodge. The different spelling reflects the names as in 1844/88.

As the population began to grow changes were afoot. The days of using tracks and footpaths to get to work were numbered, and this is clearly seen in the documents dated 1822/3. Here, a dispute involved a footway from Anwards farm towards Beachley passing quite near to Barnesville Park. The map shows the route under dispute and marks Anwards farm, but not Anwards House.

During October and November 1822 there were numerous meetings, about this problem presided over by the Justices of the Peace, as the land-owner wanted the footpath to close or be 'stopped up'. They had to consider any appeals and one in October by Timothy Lewis obviously thinks the footpath is necessary as it is 'useful to the occupiers of the Messuages, Farms and Lands belonging to me ... and to many others.' However, on 14th January 1823 the footpath is closed. There must have been some disgruntled people as a result of the decision.

Sometimes these footpaths would have stiles for access thereby removing the need to open gates. In this parish there are several unusual stiles known as slab stiles. These are estimated to be at least two hundred years old.

George Ormerod has been briefly mentioned earlier, and as he lived in the parish for nearly 50 years (c. 1825-1875) there is plenty of information about him to be found. But why did someone born in Manchester, who then settled in Cheshire, move to a fairly remote part of Gloucestershire? One reason, according to his youngest daughter Eleanor who was born here, was because the climate in Cheshire was too cold for her mother and young family. George and Sarah, his wife, had 10 children.

Another possibility may have been the choice of where he chose to live. He bought Barnesville Park, later renamed as Sedbury Park, from the trustees of Sir Henry Cosby, who had the former house built possibly on the original building or its site, namely Barnes Farm. This site looks down across the Wye into Wales, and the Severn borders the property. Coincidentally, when Ormerod lived in Cheshire the river Dee was near and again Wales was across the river.

Mention has already been made in Chapter 1 that Ormerod was an historian, particularly interested in the Roman period, as well as being an archaeologist, hence the detailed paper to Sir Henry Ellis on 24th April 1840 'Strigulensia'. In it there seems to be a difference in spelling. In the Deeds of 1499, which he quoted in his paper, there was 'a Cruce de Sedburye versus Anwelles'. This spelling seems at variance with what he mentions in the same sentence earlier, namely 'Anwells'. So, it seems the spelling of the house might lose an 'e' over time.

Eleanor Ormerod (b.1828 d.1901), George and Sarah's daughter, was a distinguished entomologist, but she also gave us interesting facts about her life in the parish. She records that it was about two miles to Tidenham Church, so presumably a carriage would be used to reach the church, except on fine summer days. She mentioned the steep churchyard, which must have been difficult to negotiate with long clothes as encumbrances. However, there were 'successive little arrangements of steps to help us up the ascent'. They are likely to be the same steps the more agile use today to reach the church. The family also had a privileged pew with curtains, in the north aisle. This was conditional, as long as Barnes Cottage, on their property, was kept in good repair.

George Ormerod, his wife Sarah and their eldest son Thomas Johnson Ormerod are buried at St Mary & St Peter, Tidenham. The oblong grave stone is clearly visible from the southern path leading to the church entrance.

There were two auction advertisements in 'The Guardian' newspaper which gave more information about local estates. The first was on 25th August 1832 about an auction to be held at the Beaufort Arms Inn, Chepstow. It comprised of Lot 1: The Tump Estate of approximately 105 acres. Summarising, it included an 'excellent residence, walled garden, 2 barns, 2 stable, waggon house, granary, cider mill, sheds, piggeries' etc. And Lot 2, The Annard Estate of approximately 85 acres, which included a 'farm house, 3 barns and suitable outbuildings…bounded by river Severn on the east. On the summit is a never-failing spring of good water, called Ann's Well'. The advert continues with 'one of the most beautiful building sites in the kingdom, on which formerly stood a large mansion.' This is proof that there was once a large house in this position, and not a farm house or cottage.

The second advertisement on 16th February 1833 is less eloquent. It was for the freehold estate of the Annard, Lewcroft, Barnards and Tump Farms of about 190 acres. Mention was made of a 'neat Dwelling-house and farm buildings.' This time descriptions of the views are made:

Piercefield, the Wind Cliff, Berkeley Castle, the Severn, the Wye, the Channel, presumably the Bristol Channel, the hills of Gloucestershire, Somersetshire and Wales.

The next topic to examine is why Anwards seems to be located in different positions on maps. The O.S. maps from 1844 to 1939, $1^{st}/2^{nd}/3^{rd}$ editions all have the location more to the south. This seems to indicate the first advertisement above in 'The Guardian' is correct, and there was no sign of the former large house in 1832. However, there was a smaller house remaining, and this must have superseded the main one in the eyes of the cartographers. There are two older maps at the end of this chapter to highlight the differences. One is marked Tidenham (Wollaston and Lancaut)-official inclosure map with award, 1815, and shows Anwards in the correct location. The second map is Tidenham tithe map and apportionment, 1843, which places Annards to the south.

There is a third map extract included, which adds much more interest to the fields by giving them names. It is also based on the 1840's Gloucestershire Tithe map. However, Annards and field number 226 Pighole both have Bn + Btn. These abbreviations mean Barn and Barton, the latter being an old word for outlying enclosure or a granary of a private estate. However, Annards, field 228, is where the earlier inclosure map shows Anwards, and field 230 for Lewcroft (House + Garden) is where Annards Cottage was. Field 225, Pighole Mead, leads down to the Severn, which will be discussed in more depth in the next chapter. Other abbreviations stand for arable (A), orchard (O), pasture (P), plantation (PL), meadow (M) and wood (Wd).

Woodland was essential land use both for timber and fuel. Hazel was coppiced to make hurdles, repair fences and for kindling, though other trees and shrubs could be used. In the previous chapter mention was made of Anwards Grove, 'coppice or wood ground' of 2 acres, and this might be part of Park Grove Wood, although there is no evidence at present.

However, there was tree planting nearby at the end of the nineteenth-century, as is shown on O.S. 1898-1939 25" 3rd Ed. At the top of Cumberland Wood (field 222) or part of Lewcroft Piece (field 231) a copse called Hussar Copse appeared. There was also approximately half of a field planted with trees, which was called Ladysmith adjacent to Pighole Mead. It is possible that the former was named after the 19th Prince of Wales' Hussars. The latter may have been to commemorate the Siege of Ladysmith, 2nd November to 28th February 1900 at Natal, being the Second Boer War.

Two small lodges are worth mentioning before considering the Census', as they give an idea of the importance and prestige associated with a larger house. The remnants of these small buildings, namely a stone wall of approximately 100 feet or 30 metres in total, are probably passed by unobserved. But this is where the two lodges to the Mead were located with a drive, track or wide path to the house. The 'wall' can be seen at the cross-roads of Bishton Lane and Sedbury Lane with the A48. Turning into Sedbury Lane the wall is on the right. The lodges are shown on the 1815 pre-Gloucestershire inclosures, the 1843 Gloucestershire tithe, the O.S. 1844-1888 1st Ed., and the O.S. 1894-1903 2nd Ed., although this map does not identify the buildings.

The O.S. 1898-1939 3rd Ed. shows no buildings, but a Bench Mark is there quite near to a very small square separate building presumably the outside lavatory. The coming of the railway meant the construction of a bridge over the railway line to allow access to the Mead.

Some sort of population surveys must have been made in the past, but as the focus is on the Anwards area the first accessible record, namely the 1841 census is the best to consider. However, it is worth a few facts about these records. They normally are taken every 10 years, apart from those of 1931 which went up in flames, and during World War II for 1941. There was a different version taken in 1939 known as a Register. One of the main reasons for this was to assess the population's strengths, ages and abilities for the forthcoming war. The census is open to the public after 100 years, although usually an extra one or two years is needed for transcribing etc. So, the next new census to be seen will be in approximately 2051.

The local census' below will only be a brief overview of the facts using head of household, family numbers, occupation and origin. The 1841 census lacks detailed facts, so if born in Gloucestershire it would be a Y, and if not a N. The later census' have more information such as number of rooms.

Census 1841

This considers the south part of the Parish of Tidenham including hamlets of Beachley, Sedbury, Bishton. However, it is difficult to understand as it shows Sedbury Hamlet, containing 57 houses, but apart from a few named houses, there are only personal names of who is there not where they live.

The nearest reference point for Anwards is at Mead House where Elizabeth Thomas, 65, of independent means and not from this county was living, along with two others.

In fact, the best way to make this census more interesting is to include the first person's surname present in the 1841 census. Starting with Sedbury Hamlet: Seys, Kitchen (Bonny Thatch noted), Davis, Privett, Morgan, Williams (Tutshill Farm). Sedbury: Harry, Jenkins, Cullimore, Thomas (The Mead), Rowland, Jenkins (who was a blacksmith so this might be Sedbury Lane), James, Pegley, Jones, Hill, Morris, Cole, Tyler, Lewis, Fryer (Badhams Court), Ormerod (Sedbury Park), Price (Buttington Lodge), Evans, Church, Miller, Kingscote (Pensylvania Farm). Then the records move to Beachley, which has 17 houses.

The census' become more informative as the decades pass.

Census 1851: Hannards. This presumably is Annards. Here was Edward Burley, 27, his wife and two children. He was an agricultural labourer and born in St Briavels.

Tump House. William Rugman, 27, with a wife, sister and child. He was a farmer of 75 acres and born in Thornbury.

There is no mention of The Mead.

Census 1861: no mention of Anwards or Annards.

Tump farm. John Rugman, 61, a wife and 3 adults. He was a farmer of 142 acres and born in Thornbury, Gloucs.

There is no mention of The Mead.

There was a Joseph Young, 69, living in a small hut who came from Charlford, which could be Chalford or Charfield, but which ever one they are both in Gloucestershire.

Census 1871: Annards. John Croat, 58, wife and 4 children. He was an agricultural labourer and born in Horsley, Gloucs.

Mead House. Arthur Clark, 31, with mother. His income was from dividends and was born in Somerset.

Meads Lodge. George White, 22, with wife and 4 children. He was born in Tidenham.

Tump Farm. John Rugman, 38. A farmer of 42 acres, born in Oldbury on Severn.

The enumerator at the time seemed determined to track every person, so after the results for Bishton he records the details of a man that slept in a barn on the night of the census. He was John Parker, 56, an agricultural labourer born in Tidenham.

Census 1881: There are two versions of the name of Anwards this time. At the front of the batch of results completed by the enumerator it says Hannards Cottage, but inside it says Annards Cottage. Edward Shaw, 66, with wife and 2 adult children. He was a farm labourer, born in Birdstowe, Hereford.

Mead House. William Jayne, 47, with wife and 2 children. He was a Colliery Proprietor, born in Llanelly, Breconshire.

Lodge, Gloster Road. Mary Saunders, 60, with son. No occupation given, but born in Elton, Somerset.

Census 1891: Annards. William Skidmore, 44, with wife, 4 children and a mother-in-law. He was a shepherd, from Whitehouse or Winterbourne, Bristol.

The Mead. Thomas Fielding, 56, with a wife and 2 children. No details of occupation and place born unclear.

Meads Lodge. John Ford, 50, with a son, widow and visitor. He was a farm labourer and born in ? Wiltshire.

Tump farm. John Rugman, 58, with a wife and 2 adult children. He was a farmer from Gloucestershire.

The effect of the railway coming to this part of the county and beyond must have had a profound effect on the population, particularly those who neither owned a horse or a carriage. Suddenly, if money or time was available it was possible to travel to places many miles away. Some may have crossed the rivers for work, but for most, home was the centre of their world for nearby work and existence. There are plenty of sources for more information on the railways. However, here are a few dates outlining significant developments.

The South Wales Railway began operating in stages from 1850, with Chepstow to Swansea beginning. Of course, much engineering work would have been undertaken before then, together with any complications to be resolved. As mentioned earlier one small construction was that of the little bridge over the railway track to connect The Lodge(s) to The Mead sometime in the 1840's. This is still in situ.

Another railway line was planned, and after some delay a spur was constructed a short distance beyond what had been Chepstow East for a short time. This spur was the Wye Valley Line with tracks to Monmouth, which opened in 1876. Tidenham station was opened in 1876 too, and later a station known as Tutshill for Beachley Halt, a request stop, was opened in 1934. The Sedbury Lane bridge over the main-line railway is approximately by this halt. Another station was opened two years earlier, namely Netherhope Halt in an attempt to attract more passengers. However, it is probable that the development of motor transport was so competitive that this station along with Tidenham and Tutshill closed in 1959. Goods traffic related to quarrying continued until the line finally closing in 1981.

The next chapter continues with the theme of transportation, but the subject is the River Severn. Anwards is considered later on, but the main evidence of routes, vessels, freight, sea levels, and other possibilities need to be examined first.

Footpath closure Anwards Farm.

Stones nr. Sedbury maybe to emphasise footpath closure.

Slab stile by footpath Sedbury Lane.

Ormerod's grave, Tidenham church.

View from Anwards site across the Severn.

1815 Tidenham Inclosures.

1843 Tidenham Tithe Map & Apportionment.

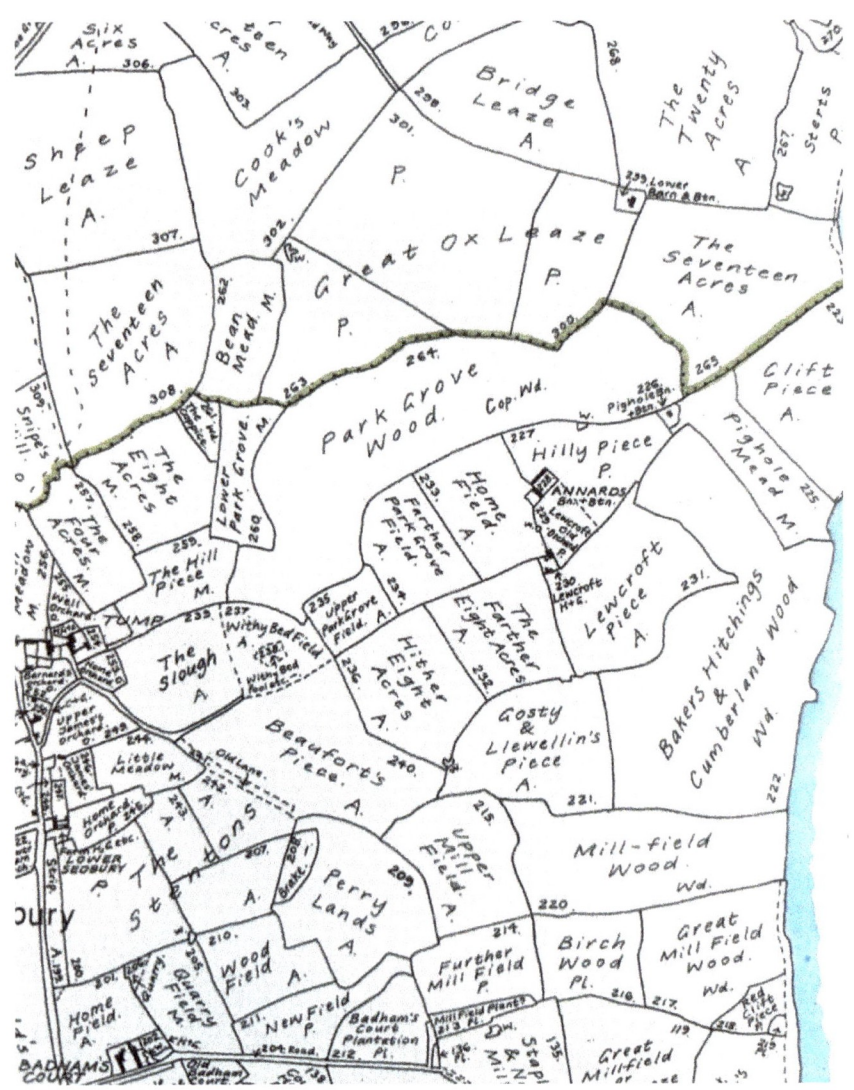

Field names 1843 Tidenham Tithe Map.

CHAPTER 5

CROSSING THE SEVERN

It is probable that the River Severn from Tidenham Parish across to the Oldbury on Severn area in South Gloucestershire varied in width over millennia. And it is likely that local fishermen would not only be using their skills to catch fish but also develop somewhat unique boats. Polynesians were able to construct boats to move between islands and to navigate the Pacific Ocean, so the necessary boat building skills were not unimaginable. In fact, there may have been communications between countries about boat building in the Bronze Age. Evidence from Norway points to the probability of skin and log boats during this period. At the same time in parts of the British Isles coracles were being made using woven branches of hazel etc. for the framework, and then covered with animal skin to make a waterproof seal. Perhaps a layer of fat may have been applied to enhance this impermeability. It is likely that these simple wooden craft were made in this area too, and that the Severn and Bristol Channel have archaeological discoveries yet to be revealed. It is known that coracles occurred on the Severn particularly in the Shropshire area, and it is probably the earliest form of boat. The first description of a coracle on the Severn occurs in 1586 (Camden's Britannia).

Left to its own device a river will naturally meander, and the Severn is no exception. The proximity of Anwards to this river would appear to be of significance, as Pighole Pill gives access directly to the Severn. Of course, it is a possibility that a charge was made to cross the estate in order to use this pill. However, it is also probable that this location was used for centuries to support the local and wider community with fish, and to move along the coast in short distances from pill to pill in small boats. Before a detailed examination is made of Pighole Pill, the earlier history of this part of the Severn is considered as it explains communication links. Indeed, it is worth noting that the Severn is Britain's longest river, 220 miles (354 kilometres), and Tidenham Parish is in what is known as The Severn Vale by The Environment Agency.

We know that the Romans were here, by the roads on either side of the Severn, the artefacts found, and the settlements discovered etc. It seems likely that apart from their mostly straight wide roads there would be smaller crossing points at various places by the river. This would remove the necessity for example of having to go to Glevum (Gloucester) to move to the east, or to go south to reach West Gloucestershire or Wales.

One of the places it is thought they probably crossed the Severn on foot or by horse, wagons and carts is from Arlingham to Newnham. One of the reasons for crossing was likely to be their need for raw materials, namely iron ore, coal and timber from The Forest of Dean. It seems this was also an ancient cattle droving point, with the distance being approximately a quarter of a mile or 400 metres. Watching the Severn Bore at Newnham as it sweeps round Horseshoe Bend, it seems unlikely anything could cross here. However, apparently there was a ford in existence until 1802 when a sand bar moved. A ferry was then in operation as shown on the O.S. 1844-1888 1st Ed., and the names Passage Road or Passage Lane in the settlements on either side would seem to confirm this route.

The Forest of Dean with its extensive iron ore deposits must have been an attractive incentive to cross at other locations on the Severn. Indeed, evidence of metal working, presumably Roman, has been founded at Oldbury on Severn, which dates from sometime between 43 AD - 410 AD. Like so many places already mentioned Oldbury seems to have other spellings to its name. There is Oldbury Uppon Severn, Oldbury Upon Severn, Oldbury with hyphens between the 'on', but probably today most locals refer to it as just Oldbury.

The Romans had part of their major settlement of Bristol at the junction of the rivers Avon and Trym. It was called *Abona* or *Abonae*, a first to fourth-century Roman town and port. It was also near another Horseshoe Bend in the river Avon, which would have given protection from prevailing westerly winds and tidal surges for their ships, galleys and smaller craft. Today, it is known as Sea Mills, with a nearby Roman villa complete with mosaic floors and a hypocaust at Kings Weston. A north-westerly highway from Bath led straight to this port. Part of the course of the Roman road is north of Clifton Down through Sneyd Park to Sea Mills, but most is buried beneath house building.

Obviously, there would have been much travel between the Bristol Channel/Severn and Caldicot Pill, which was near Caerwent, then a further distance on to the legionary fortress at Caerleon. In fact, it might be that some of the heavier goods could have been transferred to small boats and taken to Caerwent via the Nedern Brook, which Castrogi Brook earlier joined. This is not so outrageous as it may seem as the Romans reclaimed many of the levels and moors by introducing reens, sluices and embankments in this part of Wales. It would have been feasible for them to channel the Nedern/Castrogi brooks to reach Caerwent. Today, when there is heavy rainfall, there can be flooded fields to the north of Caldicot Castle, and frequently flooded fields on either side of a bridge on the M48 over the Nedern Brook appear.

Undoubtedly the sea level is rising as a result of climate change. In fact, an example of this rise is shown by a Roman villa that was excavated in Gurnard Bay, Isle of Wight in 1864. It now lies beneath the waters of the Solent. But changes occurred millennia ago, ice sheets advanced, then subsequently melted and eventually Britain became an island. Interestingly, the name of the Bristol Channel superseded its original name, the Severn Sea. This probably occurred when sea trade developed in the seventeenth-century and Bristol became England's second port.

Before considering some Roman artefacts in Tidenham Parish and possible routes across the Severn from here, there is another question still unsolved about where an event happened in the early medieval period. Much written material is hard to find, but one person The Venerable Bede (b.c. 673 AD d. 735 AD) is an authentic voice from the past. Using a complex network of contacts, earlier manuscripts, traditional stories, occasional visits to other monasteries, other scholar's letters etc. he wrote 'A History of the English Church and People' completed in 731 AD. In this book he records an event about a conference in 603 AD between Augustine, sent by the Pope, and British Christian Bishops to resolve a matter about the dating of Easter. The reasons for mentioning this is that it took place on the border between the Hwiccas and the West Saxons and no one knows where this was. Suggestions have been made that it was in the Cotswolds, at Glevum, or at Aust etc. However, could it have been at Sea Mills, formerly *Abona*? There are probably many archaeologists or other historians who would disagree about this, but the suggestion made shows that this port would have been accessible with a good road network from Canterbury via Bath, the former where Augustine was located. Some of the British Bishops based in South Wales might have crossed the water using the old Roman route from Caldicot Pill to Sea Mills, where there was plenty of woodland for large oak trees to grow by the Avon. There were many early Celtic Christian missionaries sent from South Wales to Somerset, Devon and beyond, so crossing the Severn Sea would not have been a problem. Bede tells us that the place where they all met was a place called Augustine's Oak, this surely must have been named retrospectively.

After this digression, the Romans and Sedbury are now considered. George Ormerod mentioned the discoveries made between the tumulus and Sedbury cliffs near to Sedbury Park. A variety of Roman pottery was found such as urns, jugs, plates, glazed red Samian ware as well as a kiln, various tiles and remains of lead. Ormerod suggested that it may have been a soldier's look-out over the river.

Sedbury cliffs are about 48 metres (c. 157 feet) at this point. Tidenham churchyard and the discovery of Roman coins there is further evidence that they were present in the parish.

Pighole Pill is the next topic to be examined. When exactly Pighole Pill began being used is unknown, but the Victoria County History (BHO, Glos. Vol. 10) mention Shepherdine was used in 1563 for river passage.

There was some disagreement between gentleman in the late eighteenth early nineteenth-century exploring the history of where the Romans were and the routes they used. But some think that one of the routes across the Severn started north of Oldbury, then went to Sedbury and on to Chepstow. The Rev'd Samuel Seyer in his 'Memoirs of Bristol' visited Shepperdine, near Oldbury, and seemed to have found a local guide in the area. Seyer recorded that this guide talked about old men saying 'this was the oldest ferry across the Severn, still older than Aust.' Mention is also made about leaving from Shipparden or Shipwarden '...down to a place called *pig-hole.*' The Romans on the Sedbury Cliff could easily have crossed at Pighole, thereby making it a very old crossing indeed. But there is no proof.

The next stage in examining this potential crossing was to carry out some field-work, so a visit to Shepperdine, Shipparden, Shipperdine, Sheperdine or Shipwarden, another place with many names, was needed. The first destination was Chapel House that according to records was on the sea wall in 1659. Today, it is a private house, so if this is the original house it has been modified for present times. However, the south facing wall is devoid of windows apart from a tiny one at the top, so perhaps this is part of the original house.

Using binoculars to look across the Severn towards Pighole Pill, Cumberland Wood, also known at Comeline Wood in the past, is on the left, and on the right is Ladysmith Wood. Between the two woods is a dip, which leads upwards to where older maps show the location of Anwards. This supports the possibility that this is might be one of the routes for those wishing to take their livestock across the Severn from the eastern side, and then via tortuous lanes eventually to arrive at Chepstow market. Slimeroad Pill, a short distance away to the south below Sedbury cliffs would be an alternative landing place.

Pighole Pill has a wide valley leading down to the river, and it might be that animals such as pigs, hence the name pighole, were kept in pens either awaiting onward herding to Chepstow or to Shepperdine. If tidal conditions and weather conditions were unfavourable, the sailors had no choice but to wait. In fact, it was not straight across either, as they had to cross slantways, at an angle, because of the channel of the Severn. The type of boat used is unknown, but if it was propelled by oars the tidal direction would be crucial. Negotiating the passage would have been fraught with danger with obstacles such as Oldbury Sands, Whirls End and Narlwood Rocks.

One consideration for the type of boat used in the 1500's may be the Severn trow. It is possible that the development of these boats may have come about because of the Severn mud. These trows were and are flat-bottomed, shallow draught boats, which are ideally suited to the river. This is because the internal shape of the boat is trough-like so that it can rest flat on the mud rather than listing, should the tide be misjudged.

One of the advantages of the pills mentioned is the fact that the landing places consisted of hard sand and gravel. It would be virtually impossible to discharge a cargo of animals and people by the pill entrance if it was surrounded by Severn mud, but if the tide or wind took control, using a Severn trow would mean it could settle on the mud and wait. Moreover, this is still happening today if boats are unable to move until the tide rises. This happened to a Dutch cargo ship, EMMS Servant, which ran aground heading towards Sharpness Docks in March 2024.

Cautions are given in the Admiralty Chart that the depth of water in this part of the Severn frequently changes, which means that there might be less water than predicted. The chart gives detailed information, for example south-east of Tidenham two beacons are near Pillhouse Rocks, and they are called Inward Rocks. Over near Shepperdine on the sea wall are two more beacons. One is Chapel Rock beacon, not to be confused with the beacon on the islet off Beachley, and White House beacon. Again, with the use of binoculars on a clear day it is possible to see at least one of the beacons, and an actual White House. The latter is useful for locating the correct position. Obvious places to view these would be from Poor's Allotment, Woodcroft, and Tidenham, and even from Tutshill opposite the school or Gloucester Way, when the trees are not in leaf. And surprisingly, walking down Gloucester Road just before the turning into Bigstone Meadow the White House itself is clear.

Spring tides give greater depth of water to the channel, and so heavier loads could be carried in the boats at such times. The tidal constant at Inward Rocks on a MWS, or Mean High Water Spring, is 12.2 metres, and at the White House it is 10.2 metres.

In fact, the chart shows that the depth of water to be deeper at Slimeroad Pill, than Pighole at high tide. Also, on either side of the entrance to Pighole Pill there are outcrops of rocks to be noted. But it would take longer to reach Slimeroad Pill, and possibly the land route from Pighole to Chepstow market may have been more direct.

The Domesday Book of 1086 shows that Tidenham was an active settlement with a population of 68.5 households, 67.8 fisheries, a church and a mill. It is probable there would be goods and produce to barter or sell, so Pighole passage is likely to have existed then. Indeed, salt fish was connected with this parish in medieval times, hence 'Herring Bridge' on Sedbury Lane (see Elizabeth Townley in on-line references). The fish would need to be preserved by salt and need not be sold quickly. Furthermore, Tidenham Parish offered excellent advantage points for observing neighbours and potential threats, for example from Sedbury cliffs, Beachley peninsula, cliffs overlooking the Wye and further to Lancaut.

The narrow channel from Beachley to Aust was used by ferries, but it is open to conjecture as to when the first one began. In Omerod's 'Strigulensia' he quoted that William Worcester in 1453 made comments about the distance between Chapel Rock, the islet on Beachley, to Aust being 'very inconsiderable', of no great distance, so at slack tide the attraction to cross the Severn at this location probably began in prehistorical times.

Later, it gained the name 'Old Passage' to differentiate from the new one, unsurprisingly called 'New Passage' further downstream, which probably began to operate around 1630.

The Severn silt has been a continual problem, as has been the low-lying levels adjacent to the river. The Romans and Saxons drained the soil to give easier access to widespread amounts of land using drainage channels and sluices. The resultant pasture was good for animals and this drainage work continued in medieval times. Constant attention was needed to avoid inundations at very high tides, stormy conditions and strong westerly winds. In fact, during the sixteenth and seventeenth centuries the sea defences and drainage channels needed to be managed, because if one owner or tenant was slack in looking after even a small section, the whole of the nearby community would suffer. For example, in the early 1600's a blockage caused by the Severn bringing silt, debris and gravel meant that the drainage channels were unable to drain the water into the river at 'Shipperdine's Pill', and the sluices failed to operate. Clearing these channels was costly and hard work, so fines were exacted if it was not done properly. It was the work of the Court of Sewers to decide the fines etc.

The records of the Court of Sewers list many people involved in the work of this court, as well as those who were fined or had to complete re-digging or clearing drainage channels with the risk of losing their tenancy for non-compliance. William Edmonde, a Surveyor for the Court had links with Tidenham Parish. He was a yeoman from Henbury, now part of Bristol. This may seem irrelevant, but not only was he was involved in the Court of Sewers, but he acquired a ninth share in the Beachley and Aust ferry as the following 1583 conveyance outlines. It was made between John Symmynge of London and William Edmonde of Henbury, yeoman. This transfer was to purchase a house with barns etc. and also lands in 'Bettyslye', together with a ninth share in the ferry, and Lewcrofte messuage in Tiddenham, Comerley/Lowcrofte pasture grounds and Comerlees grove. This might be Cumberland Wood. (G.A. re. D2957/306/6).

In fact, there was much buying and selling of property and lands between Bristol and Tidenham Parish around this time. The Webleys were also connected with Henbury and additionally by marriage with a Hollister as mentioned in Chapter 2.

William Edmonde was well respected as he had an important role as one of the Surveyors at the Court of Sewers. Unfortunately, he had little time to enjoy his recent purchases as he died in 1590 at 'Westburie uppon Trime'. In his will he mentions his lands in 'Beachlie' and 'Tidnam', and what seems to be 'Wraxall and Tithnam' in 'Sammersett'. Other lands, tenements and hereditaments are mentioned too, but interpreting them is difficult. Later, two of his sons Edmond and Toby were also involved with the Court of Sewers. They were Jurors between 1607-15 on the section from Kingsrode to Aust.

Another discovery revealed that the author of *Robinson Crusoe*, namely Daniel Defoe, knew about this locality. He travelled around this country in1724-6, and gave more information in his 'A Tour thro' the whole Island of Great Britain'. He had an eventful life with many occupations ranging from general merchant, prolific writer, economic speculator to spy. He mentioned that the Severn and the Wye were two great Rivers and important in the economy. Bristol merchants used Chepstow as a base to load corn into ships that were to continue to Europe. The town was an entrepôt port as its location meant it was free from taxes to the Crown, provided that the ships did not call at Bristol.

George Ormerod's daughter Eleanor has left some descriptive passages about the Severn, the island off Beachley and some sailing craft, which are worthy of mention. She compared the muddy water of the river to 'homeliness and strength'. The Lyde, which means slope and is slightly to the north of Beachley slipway, she mentioned sounded like a 'steady roar' at low tide. The noise of traffic on the Severn Bridge probably reduces that effect now. She mentioned some of the sailing vessels seen from the cliffs near Sedbury Park: schooners, barques, sloops and Severn trows. The fuel for heating their home was coal, and this was brought from Bristol in a sloop, which used Slimeroad Pill as a debarking point. In September 1838 one of her brothers watched a sailing boat from their cliffs, but 'on looking again, after a minute or so, she was gone.' It was a tragedy, as there were 14 passengers on board as well as horses, but the only survivor was a dog.

Eleanor mentioned that to communicate with Aust from Beachley, a method of signalling with a contraption that looked like a window shutter approximately two square yards to telegraph information was involved. Presumably this was to call the ferry or give information if it was delayed or cancelled.

The small limestone islet off Beachley has little precise information on who once might have lived there. It might have been a hermit, anchorite or recluse. Many names have been mentioned. There is St Twrog, a sixth-century Welsh saint. An ancient 'stone of Twrog' can be found in Maentwrog churchyard, which is near Blaenau Ffestiniog. Then there is St Tecla or Treacla, giving rise to the name Treacle Island, and not forgetting St Triog or Rioc a sixth or seventh-century Welsh saint.

It seems there was a holy well inside the refuge on the islet, and this is supported by fresh water fissures discovered when the Severn-Wye Cable Tunnel was built. There was a chapel there in 1290, but since medieval times the distance between it and Beachley Peninsula has increased, probably making the habitation difficult. It is a place fraught with danger to visit, as there is deep mud, rocks, slippery seaweed and strong currents around the islet. In fact, at particularly high tides it is difficult to see much of the islet left.

It would have been different around the mid eighteen hundreds when Eleanor and her brothers visited. The group was probably used to the Severn mud, rocks and sea-weed, and she declared that they were 'fairly safely over' on a visit. She gave the measurements of the chapel as 31 feet 6 inches long (9.6 metres), fourteen feet six inches wide (4.45 metres), with the walls three feet (.9 metre) thick. The weather conditions must have been favourable as she noted that she could 'enjoy the glorious view down the Estuary…'.

To end this chapter there is an interesting story about crossing the river, this time on foot from Shepperdine. In September 1954/5 Lord Noel Buxtun apparently walked from Shepperdine to Aylburton taking a zigzag route. In fact, it must have been very low tide, and much detailed planning would have been carried out to identify the route to take via rocks and sand bars. He must have needed a long stick and be foolhardy to attempt this. According to the anecdote he was successful, although the water came to chest height. A suggestion has been made that it was possibly a Roman ford too.

Chapel Rock Navigational Beacon, Shepperdine.

White House & Navigational Beacon, Shepperdine.

Pighole Pill sand.

CHAPTER 6

TWENTIETH-CENTURY EXTRACTS

During the research for this book, it became apparent that very few people have heard of Anwards or Annards, apart from nearby local residents. A few people had heard of Pighole Pill, either as children when they explored the wilderness and built camps, or went with their families for picnics.

Many people will be familiar with the twentieth-century, either through being born in it or having relatives or friends who were. Talking to locals to find out their recollections of this parish, together with some census information and changes to the landscape, provides the base for this chapter.

The Census' covering the years 1901, 1911 and 1911 will be examined. Again, this is only a brief overview as explained in Chapter 4. With the 1901 Census it is important to refer to other buildings as Annards/Anwards is not apparent and the order of other homes is hard to discern.

Census 1901: Home Farm. Robert Rugman, 35, with wife and 2 children. He was a farm bailiff from Tidenham.

Gamekeepers Lodge. William Dart, 31, with wife and child. He was a head gamekeeper from Chudleigh, Devon. Also in the same building was Sydney French, 22, with a wife. He was a gamekeeper from East Coker, Somerset. Could this lodge be Annards Cottage?

Near Tump Farm. John Rugman, 70, with wife. He was a retired farmer from Oldbury on Severn. This must be part of Tump Farm as he is mentioned in the census of 1891 and earlier ones at this location.

1 house not in occupation, which is not helpful.

Tump Farm. Jacob Carey Rugman, 40, with wife, 1 child, widowed mother and 2 cousins. He was a farmer from Woolaston, Gloucs.

Mead Farm. John Richardson, 80, 4 adult children, 2 others and 3 visitors. He was a retired farmer from Ireland.

Other people are mentioned, presumably along Sedbury Lane, but no details are given as to the location of their houses.

Census 1911: Meads Farm. Herbert Talbot, 35, with Head his mother, 1 child, 1 visitor. He was a farmer, and employer from Wyelands, Chepstow. The building had 10 rooms.

Sedbury Villa. Robert Burge Evans, 28, with wife and 1 child. He was an Estate Clerk on Private Estate from Sherborne, Glos? There were 7 rooms in the house.

10 Tump Cottages. Alfred Chalker, 58, with a wife. He was a labourer from Tollen? Dorset. 4 rooms in the house.

Home Farm. Robert Rugman, 47, with wife and 5 children. He was a farm bailiff from Sedbury. The building had 9 rooms.

Anwards Lodge, Sedbury Park, although on the front of the census it is stated as Annards Lodge. George Baker, 27, with wife and 2 children. He was an estate gamekeeper from Edenham, Lincolnshire. The house had 5 rooms. Later information obtained from a farmer explains there were 3 rooms upstairs, a kitchen, 2 sitting rooms, and extension to keep coal etc. There was an outside lavatory near the garden.

Census 1921: Hanards Cottage. Sydney or Sidney Harding, 31, with a wife and 3 children. He was a shephard (*sic*), farm labourer, cowman working for Mr Thomas Gaydon, Tump Farm, and from Gloucestershire. There were 5 rooms.

At the end of WWI, which would have been a traumatic time for many families and parents at home with the huge losses of life in Europe. Each death with its own history to claim. Recently, the few remaining survivors of WWII, along with military vehicles and ships were commemorated on 6th June 1944, D-Day, this year, 2024, in France and U.K.

Sometime after WWI, a decision was reached in 1927 to sell some land and buildings in Sedbury and Beachley, as it was 'surplus land acquired', probably through compulsory purchase for H.M. Shipyard, Beachley (G.A. ref. D2299/3754). There were 19 Lots, and Lot 1 was Mead House. A good description of the property together with outbuildings and land is given. The water supply came from an underground tank, so perhaps it was sufficient for the needs of the house, with a decision made not to be connected to the mains.

In fact, assuming that the description of the inside lay-out of the house is similar to what it was in 1770 when completed by William Webley, the past comes to life. Certainly, Lot 1 mentions the stone steps used to reach the entrance door, and they are still there.

Yet, it must have been the sale of these Lots, which accounts for the housing growth in Beachley and Sedbury. For example, Lot 11 stretching from the banks of the Wye on one side to the Severn on the other, with an outline of Loop Road marked, was devoid of houses. However, if the O.S. 1898-1939 3rd Ed. is examined, the probable reason for Loop Road becomes clear. In the centre of the loop is what looks remarkably like a large engine shed, and there are links of possibly rail lines coming from the south of it. Furthermore, The Beachley Shipyard is mentioned and a note beneath this it says *(In course of Construction)*, so this indicates the date of the map shown to be prior to WWI.

Between the wars and after WWII many families, friends and children enjoyed going down to Pighole Pill for outings. One person remembers swimming in the Severn, probably from the small beach where there is sand and gravel. It is a peaceful, remote location.

In 1939 a Register, slightly different from a census was made, with the focus on the age of people and their ability in time of war. Some names on the Register are blacked out as those people are still living. Properties near Anwards Cottage have been included together with a few others, as it explains what the authorities were looking for.

Anwards Cott Tump Farm

Edward B. Currey, 1910, Public Works Contractor Heavy Work

Tump Farm, Sedbury

Charles E. Guest, 1908, Dairy Farmer

16 Tump Farm Cotts

Sydney C. Stait, 1912, Lime Quarry Heavy Work

Meads Hotel, Sedbury

George D. Clark, 1879, S. African Civil Service,

  Civil Eng. Draughtsman

Jennifer Bertram, 1920, Ambulance driver Bristol A.R.P. (Air Raid Precautions)

Badhams Court, The Cottage

Herbert J. Babb, 1889, General labourer Heavy work

  Special Constable

Sedbury Cottage

John Sexton, 1891, Goods porter of JWR Heavy work

After WWII there were still reminders around such as barbed wire barricades, mines, and ordnance to explode, and even today unexploded bombs can be swept into trawl nets requiring the assistance of bomb disposal teams. Also, around the coasts and other strategic places concrete and sometimes stone structures are still seen. These are small blockhouses, or better known using the military slang, as pill boxes. There are probably many along the Severn and in this parish. There were definitely four known ones. Two at Beachley overlooking Chapel Rock, one near Snipe Hill, and one at Tutshill Recreation Ground. The latter was somewhere between Silley's Close and Ty Gwilym (formerly Tutshill Villa), although there is no evidence of that pill box now. It is possible there was also one north of Beachley slipway heading towards Lyde Rock, but no confirming indication exists.

Sedbury Park, home of the Ormerod's in the 1800's, saw a change of use when in 1941 it became Sedbury Park Approved School for Junior Boys. It could accommodate 120 boys aged 13 when admitted. In fact, there were problems there and perhaps that is why some boys absconded. Some took shelter in Annards Cottage, which is one of the reasons for its demolition. Apparently, others used trains to escape at Tutshill Halt area, where the railway line goes under Sedbury Lane bridge. It is uncertain how some achieved this if the train was in motion at the time. However, it might have been feasible to jump on open loaded goods wagons.

The Local Authority took control of this school from 1973 until 1986, and it is known that there were camping trips made into Wales.

A school at Tidenham opened in 1841 and closed in 1953. There must be records of the teacher and/or teachers and pupils, which would give more details about this place. It was located further up the village beyond the church. A former pupil remembers his time there and after school stopping by the pump in the village to have a drink of water on his way home.

As the parish grew there were changes to the road infrastructure, and when the new bridge was built it would have a significant effect on this part of Gloucestershire as well as South Wales. The Severn Bridge, opened in 1966 by Queen Elizabeth II, is an aesthetically pleasing structure. It is painted white to reflect the heat, and it manages to present an imposing yet delicate structure on grey days. However, for the Old Passage ferry it meant the end, and this also happened in 1966. It had been a vital service over the years for so many with the ferries called the Severn King, the Severn Queen and the Severn Princess. Some may remember the way that the ferry boats crossed to Aust, namely straight in a south-westerly direction, then turn 90 degrees and go straight across the river to Aust.

Anwards was also on the move, or at least some of it. Rocks from the original site was being transported to the gardens in Dennel Hill on Coleford Road. Also, at some time the well at Anwards (Ann's well) was stopped up with stone etc., as a heifer had fallen into it. This well was square shaped made of either brick or stone.

The Wye Valley Railway that had opened in 1876 closed for passenger services in 1959. With the growth in car ownership probably the demand for some railway routes declined.

Easier access to this side of the Severn increased the demand for houses. In Tutshill, Bovis built houses around the Sedbury Lane area. The company wanted to build a road through to Beachley Road, but no consensus could be reached with the planners. This is why there is a rectangular area of grass and trees hidden between Gloucester and Beachley Road and Bigstone Grove.

There was a garage by the crossroads in Tutshill, where now there are houses. Bigstone Villa or Manor was a large detached house with lovely roses in the garden. It also had some Horse Chestnut trees, and a few still remain. No date has been found for when the planning application was made for building this house, but it still exists and is listed in the 1901 Census.

Obviously, with more people moving into the area pressure would be on the A48. Imagine the route needed to be taken by car before the Wye was bridged adjacent to the railway line into Chepstow. To illustrate this, first it would have been necessary to drive through Tutshill, then taking the long curve of Castleford Hill, before stopping at the traffic lights. Chepstow Bridge, completed in 1816 by John U. Rastrick, is a single carriageway iron bridge. After this there would be negotiations of narrow roads to ascend up the high street, then under the Tudor arch, which would have been another controlled point.

Undoubtedly, change was necessary with the growth in the number of vehicles using the roads, so in the 1980's work began to construct the new A48 route from the junction with Gloucester Road to Tutshill. This would be noisy and dusty work as rock would be blasted, and the proximity and danger of trains on the adjacent railway line had to be considered too. Obviously, it would affect households living above this work in Severn Avenue. In the case of the latter, metal boxes with fans, approximate height 3 feet (90 centimetres), width 1 foot 6 inches (45 cms.) and depth 8 to 10 inches (20 cms.) were provided for the households. This enabled the residents to have fresh air circulating whilst keeping windows shut to avoid dust and noise. There is a photograph of a box at the end of this chapter.

With the opening of the road or by-pass in 1988 pressure was removed from the historic Chepstow Bridge, Chepstow and Tutshill. However, some living in Severn Avenue had to be careful with outdoor activities in the back garden, as the A48 was and is directly below the end of it.

Certainly, this change resulted in less congestion, and with this new Wye bridge built, traffic was able to flow more easily for a time.

Example of a pill box.

Chepstow Bridge with a very high tide.

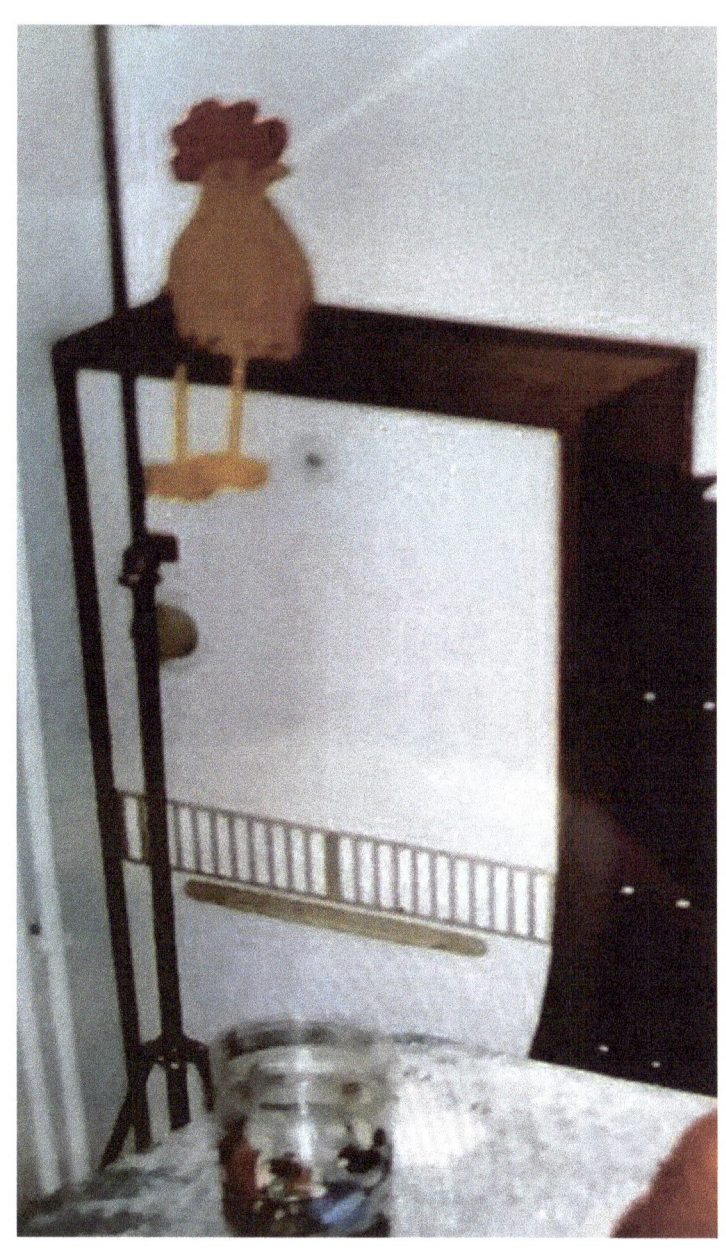

Metal boxes provided for Severn Avenue residents.

CHAPTER 7

'THE NOW SHALL OUR MORROW INSPIRE'
(Unknown lyricist/composer)

This chapter will be shorter as the twenty first-century has many decades still to complete.

Probably the most important effect on this parish was the removal of the tolls from the Severn Bridge on 17th December 2018. Tolls were also removed from The Prince of Wales Bridge at the same time. It is likely that some from the Bristol area and beyond decided to move to this parish for more space and many other reasons.

As the population grew it resulted in an increased demand for houses. This parish has seen growth in Sedbury and Tutshill, with vehicle reliance appearing to be essential. Bigstone Meadows was built around the early 2000's by Meadgate Homes from Cardiff. ButlerWall constructed Birch Grove, and Bellway built Ash Crescent estate, both around 2018/2020. Barrett's were a little later in Crane Pool Avenue, Sedbury. There is plenty more information to be seen on Tidenham Parish Plan.

These new developments are exerting more pressure on the A48. In fact, Lydney has another Bellway development in the early stages of house building. Unfortunately, even though the traffic lights are monitored, with the increase in A48 traffic, the new houses on the old ship building site in Chepstow, and consumer demand in the local supermarket, it is not surprising that at times lengthy queues approaching this junction are the result.

Yet everything ground to a halt when COVID-19 (March 2020) appeared. Initially, there were widespread restrictions until the experts had assessed the best way of tackling the disease. People adapted and walking was a good option for exercise, taking the new dog for a walk, and possibly discovering new places. Maps might have been useful for finding hitherto unknown footpaths, and Pighole Pill was found by the author using this method.

Unusual flowers were seen along Sedbury Lane, such as Shining Crane's Bill (Geraniaceae lucidun). In fact, there are other rare plants in the parish, for example, in 1948 the Rev'd H.J. Riddelsdell identified 50 violet types. One was discovered at Pighole, 'pure white flowers', Latin name Violaceae reichenbachiana.

Restrictions were gradually lifted and by March 2021 people were beginning to return to their usual life-style. But discoveries had been made, and someone noticed and shared seeing the humps and bumps by The Gloucester Way. This might be a future investigation for them. In fact, people with hobbies or interests may have continued restoration projects such as the Sea Princess Preservation Trust, or steam trains or motor vehicles.

The stretch of The Wye Valley Railway line between Tidenham to Tintern had not been used since 1981. It was an overgrown route, still with track in places and plenty of vegetation covering railway paraphernalia. Then groups of enthusiasts and volunteers came together to eventually transform the derelict track from Snipe Hill to Tintern into the Wye Valley Greenway. Much of the track, chairs etc. went to Dean Forest Railway. Other items were left in situ and the Wye Valley Greenway was officially opened in April 2021.

However, before this could happen much heavy work was involved especially in the tunnel, which at the time of writing is open from 1st April to 30th September, but this may change. The tunnel has subdued lighting the length of the tunnel, which is 1188 yards or 1.1 kilometres long. It begins at Netherhope and emerges by the Wye on the left and Dennel Hill on the right.

The surface of the Greenway is suitable for walkers, cyclists, runners, dog walkers, those with pushchairs etc. There are several seats for resting, or to listen to different birds or watch insects, butterflies and possibly mammals. The Floral Mile starts at Snipe Bridge and continues to the tunnel. From spring to autumn there is a wide range of British wild flowers blossoming during the year. The scenery is varied ranging from views across the fields looking down on the Severn beyond, or to the platform of the old Tidenham station, or the new pond nearby. Continuing onwards to the tunnel there is a section of craggy limestone rocks with Hart's Tongue Ferns in the crevices. A team of volunteers rake leaves from the paths, clear brambles and ivy encroaching onto the route, remove unwanted seedlings, and share information or general comments to passers-by.

Another group of people also got together, and this time it was to save a building that was going to be altered into two

4-bedroom houses. This was The Rising Sun at Woodcroft, which was probably first mentioned in 1858. It seems that the local community and surrounding areas were inspired by the past and wanted to save the public house.

A Community share scheme was launched to raise the necessary finance, and this was successful. The Rising Sun officially opened on 29th October 2022 as a community pub. Again, much of the work to refurbish the building was completed by volunteers, and is an example of local people joining together to achieve an aim.

The final part of this book will draw together some facts, analyse the known, introduce a subject that has not been mentioned earlier, and suggest ideas to solve at least part of this mystery.

Severn Princess at Chepstow.

Wye Valley Railway line now The Greenway.

CHAPTER 8

CONCLUSION

How can a house disappear and what did it look like? These were the initial questions that arose in an attempt to solve the mystery.

The first question to consider was did it exist in isolation? Fortunately, the indenture of 20th November 1771 between the Webley's and Thomas Nichole, (N.L.W. Citation 551), mentioned in an earlier chapter, answers this and shows the value of documents. Anwards had 'barns, stables, outhouses, Buildings & folds, Cows? Yards, gardens and orchards adjoining', so it was not a solitary house. It had land and a few field names are given as they appear on Gwatkin's annotated 1843 map extract. There was Home Orchard (3 acres), Home Close or Home Leaze (8 acres), Clay Leaze (8 acres), Grove Leaze (9 acres), Middle Leaze (8acres) and Farther Leaze or Burris's (5 acres). The need for nearby workers to attend to animals, crops and fruit may have resulted in the building of 'Annards' Cottage, which possibly increased in size later. Thanks to an invaluable source there is a photograph at the end of this chapter showing it around 1957. It is probable that the original house was adapted into large barns when it was no longer habitable or needed. Certainly the 'barn' had pantiles in evidence in the 1950/60's.

At the end of this chapter there is a sketch view of relevant named locations as seen from Tutshill in the last century.

Another question is about building materials as Anwards seemed to be a very tall building and approximately 148 feet or 45 metres above sea level. In fact, if stone was used in this house, it would have added to the time taken for construction, and much effort would have been needed by men and horses to shift heavy stone to the site. However, it could be that the original house was timber frame with wattle and daub, perhaps with stone foundations. A search through old maps has found no quarries, although on the 1815 inclosure map there is what looks like an outcrop of rock adjacent to Park Grove Wood marked. In later maps including the O.S. Explorer OL 14 of 2015, a blue small circle is now shown indicating water. Of course, there may have been an unidentified quarry around the fifteen hundreds, which now may be part of a farm, large garden or a feature. In fact, later owners of Anwards might have altered the original house, and there must be a source of stone, probably limestone here, to account for that taken to Dennel Hill in the last century. Also, there is a depression, often filled with water, in front of where the house was, so this might be a source of more stone. Alternatively, it might be an ornamental feature, or somewhere for servants to carry out their work and ablutions.

Many of the walls and buildings around this part of Sedbury are of Lower Dolomite locally known as Black Rock limestone. However, in Tidenham Tunnel it is mainly Carboniferous Limestone, so a variety of rocks are found in this parish. In fact, below Sedbury Cliffs on what is locally known as 'fossil beach', lower lias ammonites with their spiral shells and brachiopods, rather like cockle shells, are sometimes found.

Further down the hill towards Pighole Pill are the foundations of another building, identified on the annotated 1843 map as Pighole Barn and Barton, field 226. The latter word could also mean a farm yard. Later, this may have been adapted to something resembling a Dutch barn with a curved roof. In fact, the building would be a suitable place for a turnpike to collect passenger dues and even to weigh or count animals coming or going to the other side of the Severn for market. If this is fact, then this enterprise may be the original reason for Anwards house. Perhaps the owner wanted to oversee his investment.

The next aspect to consider is the source of water, a daily essential for humans and livestock. The geology of this part of the parish is interesting. Again, people centuries ago provided useful information. George Ormerod mentions in 'Strigulensia' that Sedbury Cliffs were 'new red sandstone overlaid with lias covered by transported red marle and gravel'. Certainly, movements in the rock strata has caused what was a syncline, bowl-shaped layers of strata, to be truncated by faults on the other side of the Wye. Probably later aeons deposited new strata so that almost horizontal layers were now on top of this syncline section. Anwards former 'mansion house' was on this part although towards edge of the layers. The geological name for this junction of rocks is an unconformity. This is likely to be the reason for Ann's well 'a never-failing spring of water' (The Guardian 25th August, 1832). The authority for this statement is unknown to date. However, if the public footpath is taken to reach Pighole Pill, the trickle of water on the left confirms the statement in the newspaper. It is probable that the well is artesian and rises from an aquifer in the syncline. The horizontal clays above prevent the water from reaching the surface unless a borehole is made. Perhaps a recluse or hermit in the past managed to create one, or there was movement below the surface to weaken the ground?

The next question is, who was Ann? There are other wells fairly near this parish dedicated to her name, although it is spelt Anne. At Clanna Resurgence there is St Anne's well. Trellech has St Anne's well, and also there is one at Brislington, now part of Bristol. Farther afield at Llanmihangel, near Llantwit Major, there is St Anne's well near the church, and possibly there are many other wells dedicated to this name. Hermits in the past were known to travel great distances, and probably made contact with local people and those in need of spiritual refreshment and guidance.

Another possibility is that Ann's well was there before the name Anwards appeared. Indeed, the document of 1499, mentioned in Chapter 1, refers to Anwells, so this may be the original name. It may be that Park Grove Wood to the north of Anwards house was originally Ann's wood. Anwards is likely to be pronounced this way. Indeed, there is a Welsh word which is somewhat similar, namely annwyl, meaning dear, cherished or beloved. Certainly, water would have been very dear to a recluse living alone on the summit.

To date the mystery of Anwards is not completely solved, but definitely more understanding of this 'mansion house' has been made. There are still many questions, such as who was the original owner and when was it built? It does seem there was a possible link with a place to cross the Severn, so research around the 15th to 16th centuries might provide future answers.

Anwards/Annards Cottage c.1957.

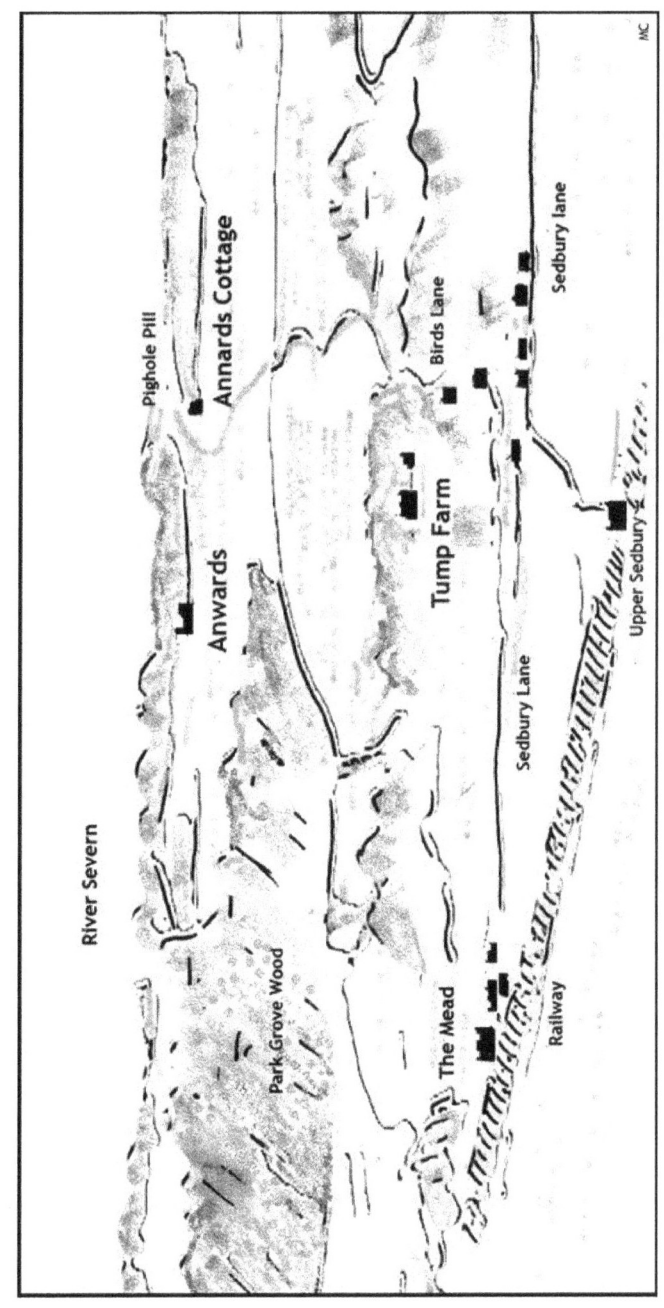

Sketch view of Anwards Location.

Pond looking from site of Anwards.

Public Footpath leading to Pighole Pill.

Pighole Barn & Barton foundations.

ACKNOWLEDGEMENTS FOR PHOTOGRAPHS

Isaac Taylor, Map of Gloucestershire 1800 2nd Edn.
(Kind permission of Gloucestershire Archives ref. MA19/24)

Plan of Lands Tutshill 1828
(Kind permission of Gloucestershire Archives ref. D1430b/30)

Isaac Taylor, Map of Gloucestershire 1777 1st Edn.
(Kind permission of Gloucestershire Archives ref. MA19/23)

Footpath closure Anwards Farm
(Kind permission Gloucestershire Archives ref. Q/SRh/1823/A/2)

1815 Tidenham Inclosures
(Kind permission Gloucestershire Archives ref. Q/Ri/144)

1843 Tidenham Tithe Map & Apportionment
(Kind permission Gloucestershire Archives ref. GDR/T1/182)

Field names 1843 Tidenham Tithe Map
(Kind permission geoffgwatkinmaps.co.uk)

Metal boxes provided for Severn Avenue residents
(Kind permission Julia & James Parsons)

Anwards/Annards Cottage c.1957
(Kind permission Keith Underwood)

BIBLIOGRAPHY

Basford, H.V., *The Vectis Report: A survey of the Isle of Wight archaeology* (Newport, 1980)

Bede, *A History of the English Church and People,* trans and intro by Leo Sherley Price (Harmondsworth, 1955)

Cave, Diana, *Saint Cedd: Seventh-century Celtic Saint* (London, 2015)

Clammer, Carol, Underwood, Keith, *The Churches and Chapels of the Parish of Tidenham: Their History and Architecture* (Tutshill, 2014)

Farmer, David, *Oxford Dictionary of Saints* (Oxford, 1997)

Hewlett, Rose (Ed.), *The Gloucestershire Court of Sewers 1583 – 1642, Gloucestershire Record Series Vol. 35* (Bristol, 2020)

Mabey, Richard, *Flora Brittanica* (London, 1996)

Loader, Rebecca, Westmore, Ivor, Tomalin, David, *Time and Tide: An Archaeological Survey of the Wootton-Quarr Coast* (Isle of Wight, 1997)

Morton, Andrew, *Trees of the Celtic saints: the ancient yews of Wales* (Llanrwst, 2009)

Ormerod, George, *Strigulensia: Archeological Memoirs Relating To The District Adjacent To The Confluence of The Severn And The Wye* (1861, Kessinger's Rare Reprints)

Rogers, Pat, *Daniel Defoe on Bristol: The Description of the City in A tour thro' Great Britain and its Context,* in Trans. BGAS Vol. 136, 2018

Smith, Nick Mayhew, *Britain's holiest places* (Bristol, 2011)

Waters, Ivor, *Turnpike Roads: The Chepstow and New Passage Turnpike District* (Chepstow, 1985)

GLOSSARY OF TERMS

Anticline	Arch-like fold of strata
Artesian well	Water, the aquifer, is prevented from rising to the surface by an impervious layer
Bushel	Capacity equal to 8 gallons (36.4 litres)
Capital or Mansion House	A name given to important properties
Clandestine Marriage	A marriage secretly performed
Esquire	Title of respect. Higher social standing
Gent	Income derived from property not work. High social standing
Gout	Channel that takes water through a structure to the sea
Hogshead	Large cask, approx. 54 gallons (245 litres)
Husbandman	Generally a freeholder or cultivates land
Messuage	A dwelling house, outbuildings and land with property for its use

Pill, Pille, Pyll, Pylle	Tidal inlet, common word in Bristol Channel & Severn Estuary
Rhine, Rhyne, Reen	Pronounced 'reen'. Drainage ditch or channel to drain wetlands close to the sea
Sea Wall	Embankment to stop sea encroachment. Made of stone, metal, natural materials, earth
Sewers	Watercourses
Spring tides	Tides immediately following new or full moon. High water at its highest
Statute acre	16.5 to the pole
Syncline	Fold in strata, approx. U-shaped
Tumulus	An ancient burial mound
Unconformity	Gap in geological record, indicating erosion, sea level change or crustal change
Warth, Wharf	A shore and low-lying grazing lands
Yeoman	Cultivates land, a farmer, may own the land

MAPS

Ordnance Survey Ancient Britain South Sheet, 1:625,000, 4th Ed. 1990

Ordnance Survey Landranger 172, Bristol, Bath and surrounding area, 1:50,000, 1993

Ordnance Survey Explorer, Bristol West & Portishead Congesbury & Chew Magna 154, 1:25,000, 2015

Ordnance Survey Explorer, Wye Valley & Forest of Dean OL14, 1:25,000, 2015

On-line:

O.S. 1844-1888 25" 1st Ed. O.S. 1894-1903 25" 2nd Ed. O.S. 1898-1939 25" 3rd Ed.

WEBSITES USED: 2022-2024

ancestry.co.uk

archives.bristol.gov.uk/records/Bk

bgas.org.uk/tbgas_bg/v129/bg129117.pdf

britishbattles.com

british-history.ac.uk/vch/glos/vol 19/pp50-52

childrenshomes.org.uk/ChepstowAS/

discovery.nationalarchives.gov.uk

fodccag.org.uk

freepressseries.co.uk/news/19236053.severn-rivers-deep-tunnel-network-pictures/

fruitID.com

forest-of-dean.net/joomla/index.php/bigland-transcripts (Ralph Bigland)

geoffgwatkinmaps.co.uk

gloucestershire.epexio.com (Gloucestershire Heritage Hub catalogue)

google.co.uk/books/edition/Memoirs_Historical_and_Topographical_of/BzUQAAAAYAAJ?hl=en (Rev'd Samuel Seyer)

gutenberg.org/files/61597/61597-h/61597-h.htm (Eleanor Ormerod) historicengland.org.uk

localdroveroads.co.uk

locallearning.org.uk/Romans/abona.html

lostcousins.com

maps.bristol.gov.uk/kyp

maps.nls.uk

murrayandblue.org/2017/06/28/Shepperdine-a-hamlet-on-the-shore-of-the-severn-estuary/comment-page-1/

nationalfruitcollection.org.uk

opendomesday.org

research-information.bris.ac.uk/ws/portalfiles/portal/34499551/411102.pdf (Elizabeth Linda Townley, 2004)

therisingsunwoodcroft.co.uk

tidenhamparishchurch.co.uk/buildings/st-mary-st-peters/gloucestershire.gov.uk

tidenhamparishcouncil.co.uk/parish-history

wyevalleygreenway.org

www.ingramcontent.com/pod-product-compliance
Lightning Source LLC
Chambersburg PA
CBHW041146110526
44590CB00027B/4142